# CUTWORK APPLIQUÉ

# CUTWORK APPLIQUÉ

## Charlotte Patera

NEW CENTURY PUBLISHERS, INC.

Printing Code
12   13   14   15   16

Library of Congress Cataloging in Publication Data

Patera, Charlotte, 1927–
  Cutwork appliqué.

  Includes index.
  1. Appliqué.   I. Title.
TT779.P373     1983      746.44′5     83–6317
ISBN 0-8329-0271-3

# CONTENTS

# ACKNOWLEDGMENT

All designs, graphics, and photography are by the author except where noted.
Models for the clothing—Dolly Owen and the author.
Thanks to Eleanor Cruickshank for helping to proofread and pointing out vagueness.

Credits for the color insert are as follows: *Primitif* from the collection of Mr. and Mrs. Donald Short. Fourth page: wall hanging, top left, from the collection of Gay Imbach; wall hanging, top right, photo by Rick Tang. *Mission Church* from the collection of Rosalene Bradshaw. *Sun Symbol* from the collection of Marian Claassen. *Unicorn and the Lady* by Kate Walker. Quilted jackets photos by Tookie McGutcheon; model on the right is Carol Boyd.

Quilt on back cover, *Summer Morning*, designed by Fay Goldey; made by Fleur Bresler, Barbara Eisman, Alice Geiger, Fay Goldey, Alice Hersom, Nancy Johnson, Mary Krickbaum, Frances Parrack, Yoko Sawanobori, Diane Smith, Jeanne Timken, and Sandra Tucker.

# INTRODUCTION

"What is Cutwork Appliqué? It looks difficult!" Cutwork Appliqué is appliqué, sewn by hand, in which your scissors are used as much as your needle. It is not as difficult as people tend to imagine. The designs are not cut until you are ready to stitch them, therefore they can not shift out of position. Basting is unnecessary. This also minimizes the fraying of pieces before you stitch them. In Cutwork Appliqué you can achieve intricate work with minimal preliminary preparation.

Some appliqué instructions tell you to turn under all the edges and baste them securely before you start working. Some will suggest pressing them under at the ironing board and even cutting templates for the shapes to aid in pressing. This is not only unnecessary with the techniques described in this book, but it is impossible.

People assume that this kind of work requires a great deal of patience. I am not a patient person. I am interested in the quickest way to get the result, which is why I believe in the simplest, most direct way of working. When people ask me how I produce so much work, I tell them that I produce what I do by not wasting time and energy on needless detail.

I have always loved appliqué for its sharp graphic quality. As a graphic designer, I prefer clean, crisp shapes and strong contrasts of color as a way of communicating. This is one reason why I have always returned to appliqué after trying many other kinds of needlework. Another reason is that precision is not one of my attributes. Appliqué need not be as precise as piecing, in which an error of a fraction of an inch can throw off the whole design. In appliqué, precision is not as important; there is more freedom of expression for me.

Another advantage of hand appliqué is the ease with which I can carry my work with me. Sewing machine work would force me to stay where the

1. If any fine white hairs are detected on any of the works in this book, Ms. Heidi takes full responsibility.

machine is, but when the weather is nice and I want to sit outside, I can carry my handwork with me.

I happen to be more adept at handwork than machine work and I find it more relaxing. I admire people who have the patience to work at the sewing machine. Contrary to what many people think, I find that handwork is less tedious than machine work. When I use the sewing machine, the fabric slides unpredictably, puckers result, and I get tired of swinging the fabric around while trying to follow an appliqué edge. People who are good at sewing machine work might find they can do the designs in this book better on the machine; however, the directions given are for handwork.

I love variety and am bored with monotonous repetition; it is natural for me to try new things. I have explored many ways to appliqué, and it never becomes boring. I have spent time exploring the mola techniques of the Kuna Indians of the San Blas Islands, located along the Caribbean shore of Panama. Do not confuse the techniques in this book with molas. They are not the same, but some of my methods are derivatives, discovered during my attempt to copy the mola techniques and then, finally, to understand them. The work in this book differs from the mola work in this way: molas are constructed within a very rigid discipline. They are made up of narrow channels of ¼ inch in width, and many outlines of ⅛ inch in width. Every bit of space is filled with detail. You will not find more than ¼ inch or ⅜ inch of space left unworked. Even the colors may be regulated. Notice the sun design that was done with reverse appliqué, compared to the mola (*photo 2*). You will see much more open space in the sun design than in the mola design. The designs in this book are much more flexible.

2. A reverse appliqué design compared to a mola from San Blas.

You can make and break your own rules. I am going to show you my favorite techniques with some patterns for you to try, and then urge you to try your own designs, or variations of my designs. You may discover some new techniques of your own.

Some of the designs are done with reverse appliqué, some with appliqué, and some are combinations. Reverse appliqué means cutting the design from the background so that it reveals a contrasting color underneath the background. The appliqué designs (those placed on top of the background) sometimes have cut-outs in them, revealing the background through a lacy open pattern. The technique of cutting and stitching is the same; it is only the placement of fabrics that changes.

If you follow the directions and colors for all of the patterns in the book, you may want to make the sampler wall hanging shown on the cover. You may prefer to make only a few of the designs, trying only some of the techniques. Remember, the designs do not always have to be put into the squares as suggested, and the patterns can be worked in several of the techniques other than the one described. You may want to use your finished designs to decorate clothing, pillows, tote bags, or whatever you can think of. There are several suggestions that you may want to try, or you may find your own unique uses.

# CUTWORK APPLIQUÉ

# 1
# MATERIALS, SUPPLIES AND PROCEDURES

2A. Charlotte's studio

# MATERIALS AND SUPPLIES

## Fabric

The best fabric for cutwork appliqué is broadcloth. I find 100% cotton (with a very fine weave) the most pleasant to use, because it behaves better when you fold it under, feels better, and I also think it looks better. In the past, when cottons were not available in many colors, I used cotton and polyester blends. I have all but abandoned the blends, but I do use one occasionally, when the color I want is not available in cotton.

The fabric must be lightweight enough to fold under and leave a crisp edge that is not too bulky. Do not use a fabric that is too heavy or coarse, because it will fray easily and be difficult to fold. There are slight variations in weights of cottons. Some are more coarse than others. They will work for appliqué but I prefer to use them for the background. There are some very light cottons that are quite flimsy with little body. These are nice to work with, especially for those corners that may be troublesome, because the fabric layers are not thick and therefore don't bunch up. Do not use a fabric that is transparent unless you are trying a special effect.

Fabric shops that cater to quilters have excellent selections. It may take years of collecting to accumulate a good supply of colors. Colors go in and out of fashion, so it is a good idea to stock up on your favorite color when it is available—it may disappear the next time you want it. It may be necessary to go to several shops; one shop rarely has everything you want.

I prefer to use solid colors in most of my designs. Although I occasionally use prints, solids give the bold effect I usually want. Prints dilute the bold, graphic quality, but if you prefer prints, use them. I also like pin dots. I find they do not interrupt my designs and add a crisp "sparkle".

# Thread

Thread quality is more crucial for sewing machine work than for hand work. I have no preference, except that the color match as closely as possible. Use your favorite.

# Scissors

This is the most important piece of equipment. Small embroidery scissors that are *very sharp* are essential. The points should also be *very sharp*, not blunt or broken off, because it is sometimes necessary to lift the upper layer of fabric by first piercing it. Sharp points are an asset.

# Pins

Straight pins are needed to hold the fabrics together as you work. You may prefer to baste, but using a few pins is more flexible. Avoid pins with beaded heads—these offer no advantage and usually catch the thread annoyingly.

# Needles

I prefer a size 9 quilting needle. The smaller the needle the better; if you like a smaller one, use it. (Remember: the larger the size number, the smaller the needle.)

# Dressmaker's Tracing Carbon Paper

My favorite way of transferring the pattern to the fabric is by tracing it with this paper. Each package may contain several colors—dark for light colored fabrics, and light for dark colored fabrics. It is sold at notions counters in fabric shops.

# Tracing Wheel

This may come packaged with the tracing paper, or you may purchase one separately. You have a choice between a plain or serrated edge. The serrated edge creates a dotted line on the fabric as you run it over the pattern. If used repeatedly, the serrated edge may wear out the pattern. The plain-edged tracing wheel leaves an unbroken line. Use whichever you prefer.

# Pencils

A hard pencil (4H or 6H) can also be used for tracing the pattern, but it may tear the paper. However, it is needed to trace the fine detail that can not be done with a tracing wheel.

An ordinary writing pencil (#2) is handy for touching up any traced lines that begin to fade as you work.

A white pencil (such as a Prismacolor) is useful for touching up any faded white lines traced on dark fabric.

# Pencil Sharpener

Sharp lines are necessary for this work, not a thick line from a dull pencil. It is a good idea to keep a pencil sharpener nearby. An electric pencil sharpener is a wonderful asset but any kind, table, wall-mounted, or a small pocket model is advised. *Keep your pencils sharp!*

# Paper

If you are not working with a commercial pattern, you will need to draw the pattern on paper. I use transparent tracing paper and I also use translucent layout paper. Pads of both of these can be purchased in art supply stores. Typing paper will suffice for tracing the patterns from this book. The patterns are full size and do not need enlarging unless you wish.

# Pen

An ultra fine-line pen is useful for tracing patterns on paper without worrying about a sharp point.

# PROCEDURES

## Choosing the colors

Choose colors *you* like that result in the contrasts you need for each design. I do not work with color sketches before I begin; I work directly with the fabric. Sometimes I cut small bits of fabric in the proportions that will be used in the design, to see how I like them. I usually select the colors, keep them together, and decide the placement as I work. Colors can fool you. They look different in a neat stack than they do in the finished piece. I always have to add and eliminate colors as the work progresses. I find it is not a good idea to cut all the fabric for a quilt at once, in case I change my mind about the color, as I work.

## Preparing the fabric

Begin by washing your fabrics to minimize future shrinking and fading.

Keep the grain of the fabrics the same. Align the pattern with the grain of the fabric.

Cut the main piece of fabric (the background) with an ample margin (larger than the pattern) to allow for finishing. Decide what you are going to do with the finished piece of work, so that you allow enough of a margin. Always allow an extra inch all around, beyond the edge of the pattern, for seaming. Do the final trimming of the seam allowance after the work is finished, because the design sometimes draws up a little, shrinking in size from the original pattern. I usually trim the seam to ½ inch when I am ready to construct the final project.

If you are going to frame the project, it is a good idea to allow 2 or 3 inches all around, so that when it is stretched for framing you have enough to grip to pull the work taut.

Press all the fabrics before you work with them.

## Tracing the Design

Place the pattern over the fabric, centering it so the margin is equal all around. Pin the pattern to the fabric with two or three pins, placing them so the carbon paper can be slipped in between. Position the tracing paper with the carbon side on the fabric. Start tracing, using a wheel or hard pencil. Run the wheel or pencil along the pattern lines. Lift up the carbon and check to make sure the image is visible. Do not be afraid to press hard. If this does not result in a clear image, you may need a more contrasting color of paper.

If you are using a light colored fabric, you may be able to see through it when you place it on top of the pattern. In this case you will not have to use carbon paper. Pin the fabric over the pattern, center it, and trace with the writing pencil.

Use a light box if you have access to one. You can see through some darker fabrics when you place them (over the pattern) on the light box.

Everyone has a vertical light box available at a window, in the daylight. Tape your pattern and fabric over the window, and trace!

# Cutting and Stitching

All the techniques in this book are similar because they all involve cutting and stitching in the same manner. The differences are in the placement of the fabrics. This will be explained in each set of directions.

After the fabrics are placed, use a few pins to hold them together. If you find that thread catches on the pins, try placing the pins with the head and tip projecting underneath, so the thread will not catch. It is not necessary to use many pins on the small patterns in this book. Three or four pins are enough. I prefer pins to basting, because I can shift them from the parts that have been stitched to those yet to be stitched.

Remember this: *Cut a little, stitch a little; cut a little, stitch a little.* Cut about 2 or 3 inches at a time. The design will determine just how much to cut ahead. You will get the feel of it, with practice. *Do not attempt to cut the whole design at once.*

The lines of the patterns are the stitching guides, to be folded under and stitched. *Do not cut on these lines.* Always add a seam allowance. The different lines of the diagrams of this book indicate the following:

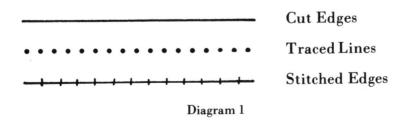

Cut Edges

Traced Lines

Stitched Edges

Diagram 1

# The Basic Stitch: The Whip Stitch

If you have ever hemmed a skirt you have used this stitch. Cut the thread to about a 25 inch length. Thread that is too long will knot and take extra movement between stitches. A shorter thread takes less arm motion and goes faster. Knot the thread. Keep the knots hidden so the back of the work looks neat and professional. With appliqué, there is a lot of fabric in which to bury the knots.

Cut the edge to be stitched with an allowance of at least ⅛ inch and less than ¼ inch. Cut only a few inches. Remember *do not cut on the line*—leave a seam allowance.

Bring the needle up on the traced line. Start in a corner if there is one; if not, start at any point on the traced line. The knot will be under the fabric to be stitched (*diagram 2*).

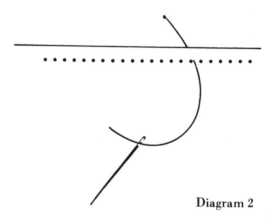

Diagram 2

Fold the edge under on the traced line, burying the knot in the fold and hiding the traced line underneath, where it will not be exposed. Put the needle into the fabric underneath, above the point where you brought it up (*diagram 3*). Bring the needle up again, through the fold close to the edge. Keep repeating this along the edge (*diagram 4*). Try to make your stitches small and close together, about ⅛ inch apart or less. The important thing is to keep the stitches as even as possible. You may want to make your stitches closer together, which is very desirable, but time consuming. Only you can decide how much time you want to take. I find ⅛ inch a compromise between perfection and time. More stitches to the inch will make the piece more durable, through washing and wearing. (This may also determine how close you make your stitches.)

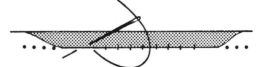

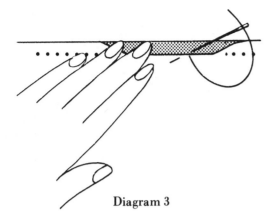

Diagram 4

Diagram 3

I prefer to work on a flat surface, usually a table top, turning the work to a comfortable position as I stitch. This keeps all the parts of the design in place and keeps the work flat. I hold the edge under, folding it toward me and pressing my left hand against it on the table until I have stitched it in place. At times it is necessary to pick the work up. I usually work on long continuous edges flat on the table and pick the work up when I stitch the finer detail. Try working this way and see if you like it. Alternate between keeping it flat and picking it up, whichever is comfortable (*photos 3, 4, 5 and 6*). When not working at a table, try a lap desk, tray, or magazine on your lap. When flying on a plane, the drop-down tray is very convenient.

3. Working flat on a table

4. Picking the work up

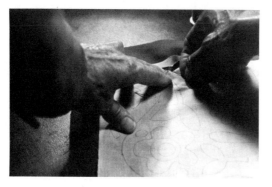

5. Working flat on a table　　　　6. Picking the work up

While stitching do not pull the thread too tightly or the fabric may pucker. Allow the stitches to be tight enough to hold but not pucker.

I always fold the edge toward me. The diagrams are shown that way, working from right to left. Others prefer to fold the edge away from them. Whichever way feels most comfortable to you is the way to work.

When fastening off the end of the thread, make a loop on top of the work, draw the thread through it to knot it. Pull the needle under the appliqué and up at some point away from the knot. Pull the thread tightly to secure the knot. Snip off the end of the thread (*diagrams 5 and 6*).

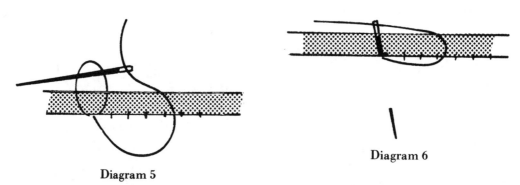

Diagram 5

Diagram 6

# Curves and Circles

*Convex curves* require a little *easing* of the fabric (fitting a larger edge under into a smaller space) (*diagram 7*). Use the tip of the needle to work the folded-under edge, keeping it smooth. As you fold it under, reach underneath with the tip of the needle and grasp the fabric allowance with the tip, distributing it evenly to avoid lumps. Press the edge under with your left thumb and hold it with your left hand as you stitch. Remember to use the tip

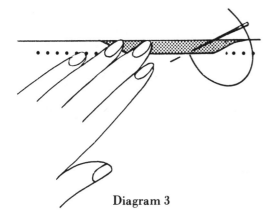

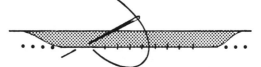

Diagram 4

Diagram 3

I prefer to work on a flat surface, usually a table top, turning the work to a comfortable position as I stitch. This keeps all the parts of the design in place and keeps the work flat. I hold the edge under, folding it toward me and pressing my left hand against it on the table until I have stitched it in place. At times it is necessary to pick the work up. I usually work on long continuous edges flat on the table and pick the work up when I stitch the finer detail. Try working this way and see if you like it. Alternate between keeping it flat and picking it up, whichever is comfortable (*photos 3, 4, 5 and 6*). When not working at a table, try a lap desk, tray, or magazine on your lap. When flying on a plane, the drop-down tray is very convenient.

3. Working flat on a table                4. Picking the work up

5. Working flat on a table

6. Picking the work up

While stitching do not pull the thread too tightly or the fabric may pucker. Allow the stitches to be tight enough to hold but not pucker.

I always fold the edge toward me. The diagrams are shown that way, working from right to left. Others prefer to fold the edge away from them. Whichever way feels most comfortable to you is the way to work.

When fastening off the end of the thread, make a loop on top of the work, draw the thread through it to knot it. Pull the needle under the appliqué and up at some point away from the knot. Pull the thread tightly to secure the knot. Snip off the end of the thread (*diagrams 5 and 6*).

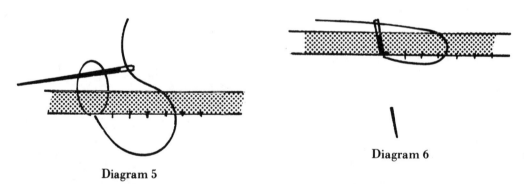

Diagram 5

Diagram 6

# Curves and Circles

*Convex curves* require a little *easing* of the fabric (fitting a larger edge under into a smaller space) (*diagram 7*). Use the tip of the needle to work the folded-under edge, keeping it smooth. As you fold it under, reach underneath with the tip of the needle and grasp the fabric allowance with the tip, distributing it evenly to avoid lumps. Press the edge under with your left thumb and hold it with your left hand as you stitch. Remember to use the tip

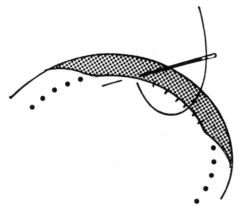

Diagram 7

of the needle to get rid of unwanted points. Try to keep the edge smooth. (Don't be too hard on yourself if you have a few points—it happens to all of us.)

*Concave curves* require clipping to make the edge fold under. The number of clips is determined by the size of the curve. Large curves require fewer clips, small curves require more (*diagrams 8 and 9*). After you have clipped, place your needle farther along the edge and twirl it toward you in one sweeping motion, turning the whole edge under in one stroke (*diagram 10*). Hold it under, and start stitching. This is fun, not difficult!

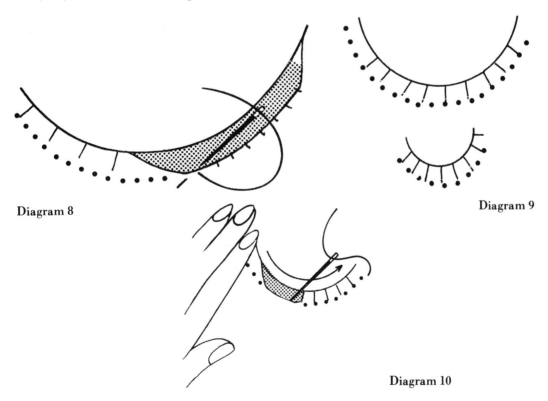

Diagram 8

Diagram 9

Diagram 10

# Corners

*Outward corners* produce a little bulk. To get rid of some of the extra bulk, trim off the corner. Fold one side under and stitch to the corner. Place an extra stitch right at the corner to keep it well anchored in place, while you fold the other edge under (*diagram 11*).

On a very long sharp point, trim a little more off of the edge nearest the point (*diagram 12*). These are the most troublesome corners. By trimming off more, you make the job easier. Don't trim too close to the edge or you will have nothing to turn under. Work the same way, with two stitches at the point. Place a few extra stitches near the corner, as needed. It may be helpful to moisten the corner to make it more manageable.

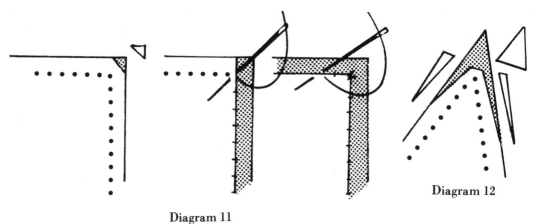

Diagram 12

Diagram 11

*Inward corners* must be clipped right into the corner. Do not be afraid to clip to the corner points. Fold the edge under and stitch to the corner. Place an extra stitch in this corner also and push any frayed threads under. Continue stitching away from the corner (*diagram 13*).

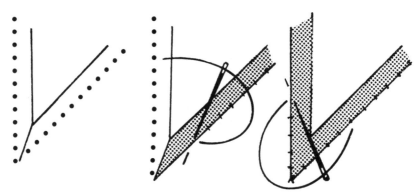

Diagram 13

Remember, you will seldom see a perfect sharp corner in appliqué work. Don't try to do the impossible. The technique has its limitations. It takes practice! There are two kinds of viewers: the intuitive feeling types who see the overall design and color before the workmanship, and the analytical thinkers who see only details. Only you can decide which is the most important.

# Pressing the Finished Work

Place a folded towel several layers thick on the ironing board. Turn the work over and press the back of it on the towel. This will remove wrinkles without flattening the appliqué completely.

Mark seam lines on the back of the work along with the allowances. Trim off any excess fabric.

# Hints

1. Try to avoid frayed edges.
2. Strive for small, even stitches.
3. Matching thread color will help to hide uneven stitching.
4. Use moisture on stubborn corners.
5. Don't be afraid to push and shove with your needle tip to turn those bulky corners.
6. If a corner is too bulky, trim off as much as you can.
7. As you work, keep turning the piece so it is comfortable, keeping your hands in a natural position. Do not try to work in an awkward position.
8. The directions for the patterns in this book are given in the colors that were used in the wall hanging on the cover. Feel free to substitute colors as desired.
9. Use a thimble if you are used to one.
10. Don't forget: it takes practice!

# 2
# CUT-AS-YOU-GO
# APPLIQUÉ

7. Pattern 1

8. Pattern 2

In a typical piece of appliqué, you may work on a design composed of simple shapes (such as a tulip, leaf, stem, heart, or circle) cut from different fabrics (*diagram 14*). In this case, it makes good sense to cut each piece, position all of the pieces on the background, and stitch them in place.

But what if you would like to put these shapes together and cut them all from one piece of fabric? (*diagram 15*). Or maybe you would like to cut a series of shapes from the same fabric or color and place them so they are not touching, but are in close proximity to each other (*diagram 16*). In both of these instances, it makes more sense *not to cut the entire design at once.* If you do, you will have to keep all those parts in position with basting. As soon as you cut them, they begin to drift out of position. The procedure is simplified by *not cutting them until you stitch them permanently.*

This method works well for lettering (*photo 9*) or for any design that is cut from one piece, but has many parts projecting from it. Notice the leaf parts on the blocks in this quilt (*photos 10 and 11*). They were cut from one piece of fabric for each block, a little at a time, and stitched between cuts. After they were completed, other details were appliquéd in place, to finish the design—the vase, flowers, and the bird. The four-corner oak leaf design, which is a folded cut paper design, was cut and stitched the same way.

Begin by tracing the design to one piece of fabric (*diagrams 17 and 18*). Pin it to the background fabric with two or three pins. Instead of cutting the entire work at once, cut only a few inches, stitch that much, and cut some more (*diagram 17*). Continue to work until you are back to your starting place. No matter how complex your design is, it is not difficult to appliqué if you delay your cutting. This tree design is in the process of being cut and stitched (*photo 12*).

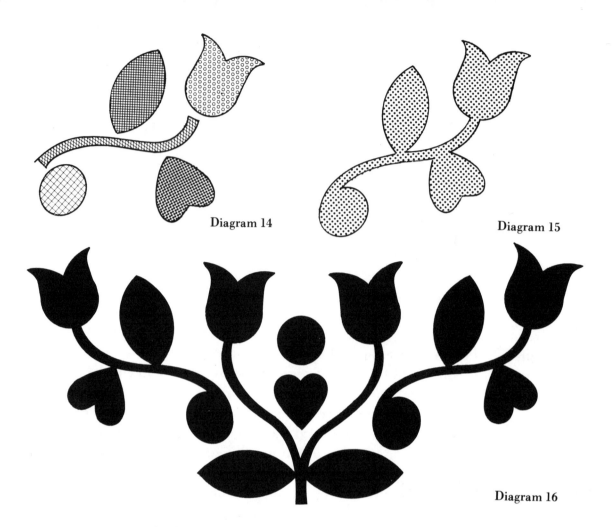

Diagram 14

Diagram 15

Diagram 16

9. Lettering is easy with cut-as-you-go appliqué.

10. The leaf parts on these quilt blocks were traced to and cut from a solid piece of fabric with cut-as-you-go appliqué.

11. The four corner oak leaf design was cut and stitched the same way.

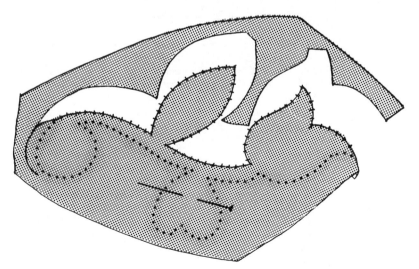

Diagram 17

**21**

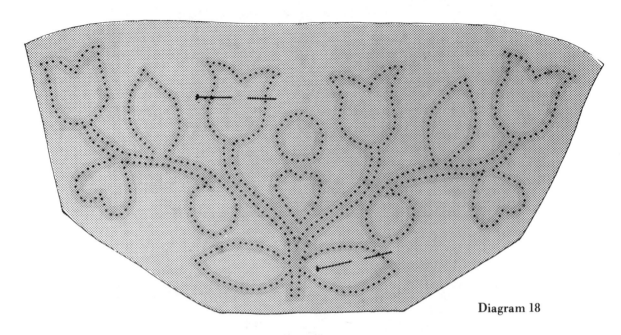

Diagram 18

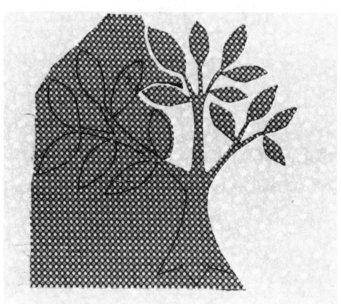

12. This tree design is in the process of being cut and sewn.

# Pattern 1

Materials: 9 inch square of burnt orange cotton broadcloth; 7½ inch square of dark wine cotton broadcloth; dark wine thread

1.  Trace the pattern on a piece of typing paper. Tape the paper over the page and trace with a pencil.

2.  Pin the traced pattern over the dark wine square, centering it. Place dressmaker's carbon paper (white or a light color) between the pattern and fabric with the carbon side down on the fabric. Trace the design with a wheel or hard pencil. Remove the paper.

3.  Center the traced wine square over the burnt orange one, pinning it with two or three pins. (I find students sometimes using twelve or fifteen pins for a design like this, but two or three are adequate.)

4.  With scissors, start at the bottom of the stem and cut the fabric ⅛ inch away from the traced line. Cut part way around the tulip. Clip the inward curve.

5.  Start folding the edge under and stitching the edge, making small, even stitches.

6.  Clip, as necessary, at concave curves and into the inward corners (*diagram 19*). This shows the cutting procedure. In the narrow space between the tulip and the stem, slit only. Do not cut away any fabric there. When the space begins to widen, cut away fabric as necessary.

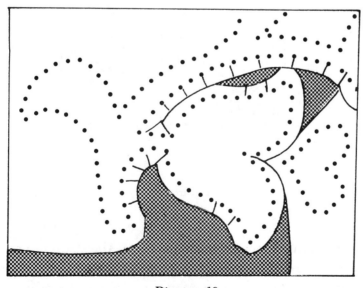

Diagram 19

7. Continue cutting and stitching. As you cut, the small heart and two circles will be cut loose. Keep them pinned in position until you start a new thread. Cut and stitch each one individually and remove the pin (*diagrams 20 and 21*).

8. Work all the way around the design to the starting place, then cut and stitch the loose flower (*diagram 22*).

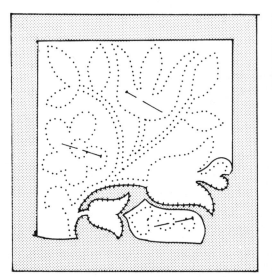

Diagram 20

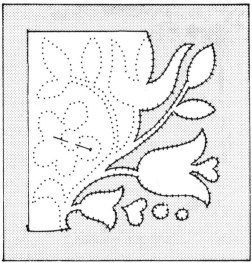

Diagram 21

Diagram 22

9. Press the design as described in chapter one. Mark seam lines on the back to form an 8 inch square. Measure a ½ inch seam allowance, mark it, and trim on the allowance. The design is now ready to piece to the other squares.

This technique is useful for unlimited designs. This sun panel was made in the same method (*photo 13*). This is how the sun looked when it was half completed (*diagram 23*).

13. Sun Panel

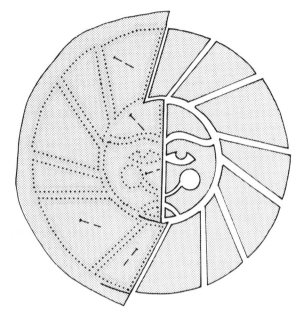

Diagram 23

To form a round panel like this, stretch the finished circular design over a macrame ring. Macrame rings are available at craft supply stores. They come in varying diameters. When your round design is ready to stretch, trim it with an extra 1½ inch beyond the edge of the ring size. Gather it around the edge with a very strong thread, such as button and carpet thread. Place the design over the ring and pull the thread very tightly, securing it around the ring. Tie it and knot it. If it needs further tightening, criss-cross the thread to opposite edges, to bring them toward the center. Pull them tight. Repeat two or three times, as needed. Finish off the back by stitching another circle of fabric over it. Attach a loop to the center-back top, for hanging.

These experimental Russian dolls were also made with the same appliqué technique (*photo 14*). This is how they were stitched with the cut-as-you-go method (*photos 15 and 16*).

This quilt block made by Marie Robertson, for my *Sun Friendship Quilt*, is another example. The rays of the sun were drawn on the light print, pinned over the dark dot foundation fabric, and stitched one at a time after each was cut. When the rays were completed, Marie added other parts of the design (*photo 17*).

14. Two experimental Russian dolls

15. First doll being cut and stitched

16. Second doll being cut and stitched

26

17. *Sun Friendship Quilt* block by Marie Robertson

Cutting folded paper is a delightful and easy way to make a design that is your own. Cut a square of paper to the size you want the design to be. Fold it in half, and fold it in half again. Fold it diagonally from the center point of the original square (indicated by the dot) to the four corners (*diagram 24*). Start cutting, with your scissors for cutting paper. Keep it simple. Open it up and see what you get! You may have a design for a new quilt block. If you don't like it, throw it away and try another or try *Pattern 2*.

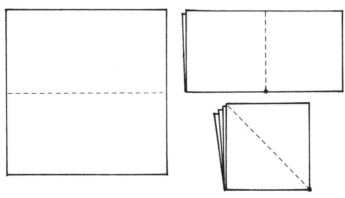

Diagram 24

# Pattern 2

Materials: sheet of typing paper; 9 inch square of golden yellow cotton broadcloth; 7½ inch square of magenta cotton broadcloth; magenta thread

1. Cut the typing paper to a 7 inch square. Fold it as shown above.

2. Open the square and place it over the pattern. You will be able to see the pattern through the paper. Line up the center point of the square with the center of the design, and the fold lines with the broken lines of the pattern. Trace the solid line of the pattern with a pencil. When unfolded, the dotted lines of the pattern indicate how the pattern looks.

3. Fold the paper again. With scissors for cutting paper, cut along the traced line (*diagram 25*). Open the square. Four sections of the paper will have dropped away. Take the one with the circle marked on it and cut it out on the fold. Save it.

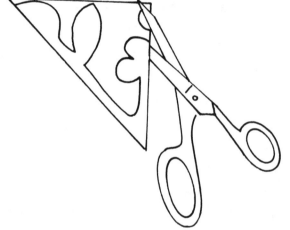

Diagram 25

4. Center the pattern over the magenta square, and pin. With a writing pencil, trace around the edge of the pattern. Remove the paper pattern. Position the circle on the magenta square following the pattern and trace around it four times, as indicated by the design.

5. Center the magenta square over the yellow one and pin. Start cutting ⅛ inch away from the traced line and start stitching it under in the same cut-as-you-go method as *Pattern 1*. Keep moving the pins from the stitched parts to the parts to be stitched. Keep the circles pinned until they are stitched (*photo 18*).

6. Press and trim as in step 9 of *Pattern 1*.

18. Keep circles pinned until they are cut and stitched.

# Hints

1. Look in books about stencil design for ideas.
2. Keep the parts of your design at least ¼ inch apart, to allow enough for turning under.
3. Do not let details get too tiny. Keep it simple.
4. Some appliqué workers place pins around the edge of the appliqué piece every ½ inch after turning it under. This is not necessary. Work only 1 inch or so at a time.

Diagram 26, decorative design ideas

# 3
# OPENWORK
# APPLIQUÉ

19. Pattern 3

20. Pattern 4

Now that you have learned how to appliqué any shape, no matter how complex, by cutting-as-you-go, there will be times when you will want to have cut-outs within a shape. They can lend a very lacy, interesting, and decorative look to a simple appliqué shape. Many people refer to this as "reverse appliqué," but I do not. Reverse appliqué happens when the *background* is cut to reveal fabric underneath it. In "openwork appliqué" the *appliqué shape* is cut to reveal the background underneath it.

In the last chapter we took a look at a piece of lettering which did not happen to have a letter with an opening in it—I LIKE STITCHING. Most words contain open letters. Here is a sign that I use to justify the usual clutter in my studio (*photo 21*). The words were divided into four parts, each a different color. Each letter was cut from paper. The letters were then laid out together and drawn on a sheet of layout paper, then each set of words was traced on a different color of fabric. Each of these four fabrics was positioned and stitched, one at a time, as shown in these step-by-step photos (*photos 22, 23, 24, and 25*).

Here are two more cut folded paper designs from the quilt shown in chapter two (*photo 26*). Each of these has a shape cut from the center, revealing the printed fabric in the background.

Just for fun, try a few more designs cut from folded paper, as shown in chapter two. This time, incorporate some lacy cut-outs (*photo 27*). This shows some cut paper patterns. Most have cut-outs in them, but the upper two do not.

I decided to try a larger cut paper design for the front of this dress (*photo 28*). The dress features a large front panel positioned on the bias of the fabric. I needed a square design that measured 24 inches. I cut a square of paper to that size. After folding it, I sketched in a design on one-eighth of it. I cut it, opened

21. Studio sign

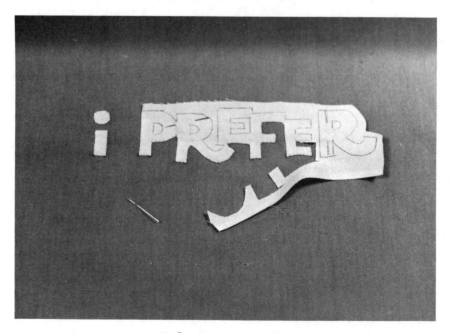

22. Studio sign, step 1

23. Studio sign, step 2

24. Studio sign, step 3

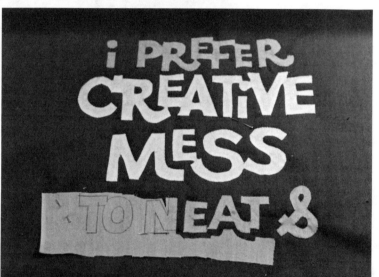

25. Studio sign, step 4

26. Two more quilt blocks with cut folded paper designs

27. Cut folded paper designs, ideal for quilt making

28. Dress with large cut folded paper design

**New Guinea Images** *(Reverse appliqué)*

**Natureforms** *(Stained glass reverse appliqué)*

**Reflections** *(Positive and negative appliqué)*

**Twilight** *(Positive and negative appliqué)*

**Dawn** *(Positive and negative appliqué)*

Sun design *(Cut-as-you-go appliqué)*

Russian dolls *(Cut-as-you-go appliqué)*

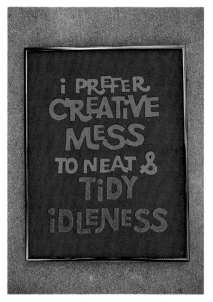

Studio sign *(Cut-as-you-go appliqué)*

Tote bag *(Openwork appliqué)*

**Primitif** *(Cut folded paper design)*

Butterfly *(Cutwork appliqué)*

Dress *(Cut folded paper design)*

Wall hanging *(Stained glass reverse appliqué)*

Wall hanging *(Stained glass reverse appliqué)*

Wall hanging *(Stained glass reverse appliqué)*

Design with print fabrics *(Stained glass reverse appliqué)*

**German Village** *(Stained glass reverse appliqué)*

**Christmas Star** *(Stained glass reverse appliqué)*

Vest *(Stained glass reverse appliqué)*

Dress *(Stained glass reverse appliqué)*

**Reflections** quilt block *(Negative appliqué)*

**Reflections** quilt block *(Positive appliqué)*

The Author's logo *(Reverse appliqué)*

Dress *(Reverse appliqué)*

**Primal Fish** *(Reverse appliqué)*

**Mission Church** *(Positive and negative appliqué)*

**Sun Symbol** *(Reverse appliqué)*

Tote bag *(Reverse appliqué)*

Items made with *reverse appliqué*

Pillows *(Reverse appliqué)*

Wall hanging *(Reverse appliqué and appliqué)*

Madonna *(Reverse appliqué)*

Garden of Eden *(Reverse appliqué)*

**Unicorn and the Lady** *(Reverse appliqué)*

Two quilted jackets with inlay appliqué medallions (fronts and backs)

it, and decided to use it on the dress (*photo 29*). It fit nicely on a card table, so that is what I worked on. I transferred the pattern to a piece of gold fabric, pinned it to the dress panel, and started to work (*photos 30, 31, 32 and 33*). I started with the inside portion, then skipped to the inner edge of the outside piece, and then to the outer edge. After finishing the outer edge, I came back and finished the inner edges. I then made the dress and decided I liked the design well enough to use it on a quilt in the future (*diagram 27*).

This relates, in a way, to the Hawaiian quilt designs, although Hawaiian quilters prefer to cut the entire design and then baste it carefully. If you find

29. Cut folded paper pattern used on the dress

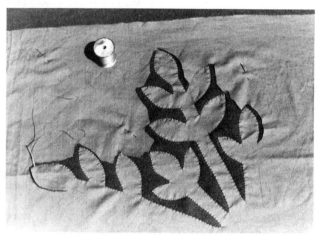

30. Part of the inner portion stitched

31. Inner edge of the outer portion, partly stitched

32. Outer edge of the outer portion, partly stitched

33. The entire design, partly finished

Diagram 27

*38*

basting as tedious as I do, then try your next Hawaiian quilt using this "cut-as-you-go" method. I have never made a design like this as large as a bed quilt. To do a design that size would require basting as pins would never stay in place, but it would not require the meticulous basting that most Hawaiian quilters do.

There are quilts made in Pakistan that feature cut folded paper designs. This tote bag (*photo 34*) was inspired by one of those designs. The green square was appliquéd to the magenta square. All the lacy parts were then cut from the green square and stitched to reveal the magenta square underneath. Orange strips were added to the edges for the front of the bag.

This cut folded paper idea does not have to be limited to four-pointed designs. How about a six-pointed snowflake, like the one on this hexagonal wall panel? (*photo 35*). Take a square of paper, fold it in half, and fold it two more times to form an equilateral triangle (*diagram 28*). Fold it in half again. Start cutting, making sure you cut where there are twelve layers of paper, as

34. Tote bag with a cut design inspired by a quilt from Pakistan.

35. Hexagon snowflake panel

indicated by the arrow. If you cut above that, some of the design will be missing when you open it. Snowflakes have many wonderful shapes. Start looking at some and cut your own. You may want to make a snowflake quilt.

This hexagonal panel was made by first piecing together four squares of blue and turquoise fabrics. The snowflake was appliquéd to the center where the four pieces meet, then the whole piece was quilted. This was stretched over a hexagonal macrame form, stretched, and finished the same way as the sun panel in chapter two. A series of snowflake panels like this would be a nice addition to the wall of a mountain cabin.

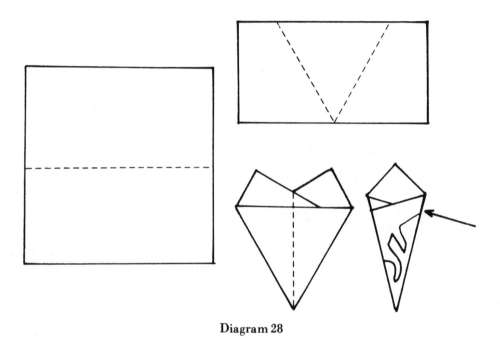

Diagram 28

# Pattern 3

Materials: sheet of typing paper; 9 inch square of olive green cotton broadcloth; 7½ inch square of golden yellow cotton broadcloth; golden yellow thread

1. Follow steps 1 to 3 given in chapter two, *Pattern 2*. Discard the cut away parts.

2. Center the paper design over the golden yellow cotton square, and pin. With a writing pencil, trace around the edge and around the openings of the design. Remove the paper pattern (*photo 36*).

36. Trace around the edge of the paper pattern on the fabric.

3. Center the yellow square over the olive one, and pin. Start cutting ⅛ inch from the drawn line of the outer edge and start stitching it under in the same way as *Pattern 2 (photo 37)*.

4. To cut the openings, pierce the center of the opening with the tip of your scissors *(diagram 29)*. Lift up the appliqué, and cut. Scissors with sharp points are essential. Cut and clip the small openings *(diagram 30)*. Do not remove any fabric from the small shapes.

5. Stitch the edge of each opening, working on one at a time.

6. Press the design as described in chapter one. Mark the seam lines on the back to form an 8 inch square. Measure a ½ inch seam allowance, mark it and trim on the allowance. The design is now ready to piece to the other squares.

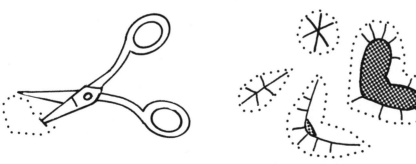

Diagram 29                    Diagram 30

37. Pattern 3, partly cut and stitched

This work, entitled *Primitif* was made of assorted cut paper designs. They were cut from five different colors of olive and gold (*photo 38*). Some of the designs were rectangles instead of squares, folded only twice. The four-corner designs were cut with compound folds, meaning the folding process was in several places in the rectangles. Spirals were cut from two of the parts, after the edges of the parts were sewn down. All of these parts of the work were cut-as-you-go appliqué. The work was inspired by a design I had seen from India. I finished the design with rick rack around the edge. You may think that cut folded paper designs are given to children for play exercises. Sometimes it pays to allow yourself to play like a child. Try it! You may come up with something special.

# Pattern 4

Materials: 9 inch square of olive green cotton broadcloth; 7½ inch square of hot pink; hot pink thread

1. Trace the pattern to a piece of typing paper. Tape the paper over the page and trace with a pencil.
2. Center the traced pattern over the hot pink square, and pin. Place

*38. Primitif*
Collection of Mr. and Mrs. Donald Short
Photo by George Rickman

dressmaker's carbon paper (dark enough to show the image on the pink fabric) between the pattern and fabric with the carbon side down on the fabric. Trace the design with a wheel or hard pencil. Remove the paper.

3. Center the traced pink square over the olive one, anchoring it with two or three pins.

4. With scissors, start cutting a ⅛ inch allowance around the traced line. Start stitching it to the background, cutting as you go.

5. Now start working the inside cut-outs, cutting or slitting them and stitching them down one at a time as in steps 4 and 5 of *Pattern 3*. (*photos 39 and 40*).

6. Finish off the square as in step 6 of *Pattern 3*.

The butterfly design in this wall hanging shows how cut-outs can enhance a simple shape (*photo 41*). The wings of the butterfly were drawn on a piece of dark yellow fabric. They were pinned over a lighter yellow and appliquéd, edges first and then the cut-outs. The wings were then appliquéd to the striped background. The body of the butterfly was then placed on top and appliquéd. The whole butterfly was then defined with a strip of bias tape, stitched all around.

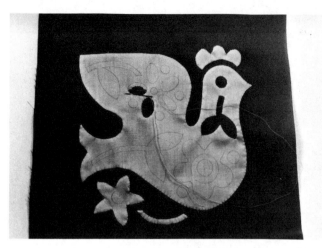

39. Pattern 4, small openings being cut and stitched

40. Pattern 4, more openings completed

41. *Butterfly*

44

Cut-out details do not have to be complex. My *Sun Friendship Quilt* has this addition made by Dottie Zagar (*photo 42*). It is a charming orange sun appliquéd to a yellow square. The cheeks, eyebrows, and the circle defining the center of the sun were cut out, revealing the yellow background underneath. Dottie then embroidered the fine facial details.

My *Sun Friendship Quilt* was made for me by a group I belong to known as the "Stitchin' Bitches" (*photo 43*). We have already looked closely at two of the

42. *Sun Friendship Quilt* block by Dottie Zagar

designs. In a later chapter we will examine two more of the blocks. After I received the blocks from my friends, a little poem popped into my mind and I decided to add it to the quilt. The lettering was done the same as the lettering shown in the early part of this chapter. It was divided into eight parts and each part was traced to a different piece of fabric. Then two sets of words on two fabrics were done on each of four blocks. Lettering comes in very handy for banners and quilts, especially when you want to commemorate an event.

**43.** *Sun Friendship Quilt* made by The "Stitchin' Bitches": Dena Canty, Jane Le Ellis, Karin Greenwald, Hope Hightower, Charlotte Patera, Pat Patterson, Marie Robertson, Peg Tetlow, Kate Walker, Frieda Walters and Dottie Zagar. Quilted by Charlotte Patera. Photo by Sharon Risedorph and Lynn Kellner

Diagram 31, decorative design ideas

# 4

# SIMPLE REVERSE APPLIQUÉ

**44. Pattern 5**

At this time, reverse appliqué is treated as a technique that is very compli-cated, exotic, and tedious. The big surprise is that it is no different from regular hand appliqué. Edges are cut with an allowance, folded under and stitched down just the same as in any other appliqué. Curves, corners, and points exist in both. There is really very little difference. Some people are surprised to learn that often it is actually easier. This is surely true of circles. The only difference between the two is that the design appears to be "incised" in the fabric instead of "added on." It can give an interesting "carved" look.

Frequently, the term, reverse appliqué, is equated with the molas of the Kuna Indians of Panama's San Blas Islands. The molas that they make to wear on their blouses have become well-known as exercises in reverse appliqué. This concept is not quite accurate because many molas contain more appliqué, which is just as remarkable, than reverse appliqué. The rich delicacy of the appliquéd parts of the mola has been overlooked, as most viewers stress the reverse appliqué, following the popular notion.

The parts of the mola that are done as reverse appliqué are slit only. Large masses of fabric are seldom cut away and removed (*diagram 32*). An outline defining a shape is slit and stitched on both sides to form a narrow channel which defines a shape or figure. This shape is always the same color as the background, separated by the narrow channel (*diagram 33*). (Sometimes there is a rare variation in which the figure is not the same color as the background, if two matching molas have been cut simultaneously of two colors with certain parts transposed.)

All molas are begun with these narrow channels either defining figures or meandering in maze-like patterns. If three or four layers are used, they are added on top of the lower ones which remain visible only as narrow outlines adjacent to the original channels. Molas are *not* cut from the top layer down, as

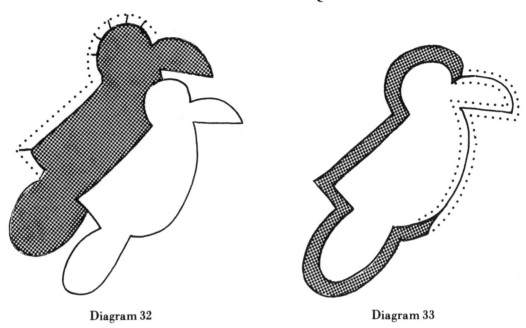

Diagram 32                    Diagram 33

everyone who is not a Kuna Indian seems to believe. Unfortunately, the Kunas, the true experts on their techniques, do not write books. Outsiders who do write books seldom make molas. The Kunas would probably snicker over most writers' explanations of how they do their work. (This includes some of my previous writings.)

Another use of this slitting technique is to fill-in space with small repetitive patterns. All other detail is appliquéd with one piece over another piece so that each under piece is seen as an outline around the upper one.

It is possible that reverse appliqué was invented through a naive attempt to explain how molas are made. This attempt was fortunate, because it has opened a new way for fabric artists to express their ideas. However, reverse appliqué had probably been around before molas had been discovered and removed from their origin. Currently, the Hmong refugees from Laos are introducing to us their work with similar reverse appliqué detail. Some of it bears a close resemblance to mola work.

Both of these types of appliqué are appreciated for their tiny detail. Not all reverse appliqué has to include such minute work. In this chapter we will work on a simple bird design in two colors. Then I will show you ways to add more color to the same design.

In regular appliqué, pieces are cut and sewn to the top of the background fabric. In reverse appliqué, pieces are applied under the background fabric which is cut and stitched down to them. In a later chapter, we will learn how to achieve more depth. Now we will learn about reverse appliqué in its simplest form with *Pattern 5*.

# Pattern 5

Materials: 9 inch square of dark wine cotton broadcloth; 7½ inch square of light olive green cotton broadcloth; wine thread

1. Trace the pattern to a piece of typing paper. Tape the paper over the page and trace with a pencil.

2. Center the traced pattern over the dark wine square, and pin. Place dressmaker's carbon paper (white or a light color) between the pattern and the fabric with the carbon side down on the fabric. Trace the design with a wheel or hard pencil. Remove paper.

3. Pin the traced wine square over the olive one, making sure the olive covers all parts of the design from behind. Hold it up to the light to check.

4. With your scissors, pierce one of the parts of the design inside the traced line. It doesn't matter where you begin, but let's begin with the wing (*diagram 34*). Cut inside the line with an allowance of ⅛ inch. Discard the cut scrap (*diagram 35*).

5. Fold the edge of the wing under, and stitch it.

6. Continue with all parts of the design. Remember to cut only a little at a time and stitch a little. The less you pre-cut, the more stable the design will remain while you work on it.

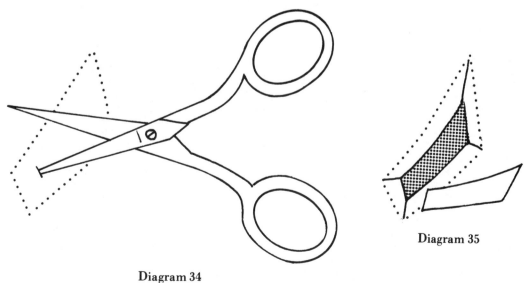

Diagram 35

Diagram 34

7. When you do the eye of the bird and the center of the middle flower, keep them pinned in place after you have cut and stitched the bird's head and the flower around the outer edge. Then cut them with the usual allowance and stitch them down (*diagrams 36 and 37*). In other words, "appliqué" them in place.

8. Work all parts until it is finished. Cut the tiny circles on the left as shown in chapter three. You may now agree with me that circles are easier with reverse appliqué than with regular appliqué. Remember to keep using your needle tip to push the edges under in place.

9. Press the design as described in chapter one. Mark seam lines on the back to form an 8 inch square. Measure ½ inch seam allowance, mark it and trim on the marked seam allowance. The design is now ready to piece to the other squares.

Most of the designs in chapters two and three could be made with reverse appliqué. Here is the sun design showing how it could have been made with reverse appliqué (*diagram 38*).

Reverse appliqué can be a wonderful way to add decorative detail to a piece of clothing. One of my favorites is this long vest, cut following a style worn in the Epirus section of Western Greece as part of their regional costume (*photo 45*). After cutting the pattern for the vest, I ignored the traditional fabric (heavy black wool) and the motifs from the region, traditionally embroidered in red. I used my own favorite light cotton and my own motifs. The lining of the vest is a navy blue homespun rayon fabric. I used a russet and red cotton

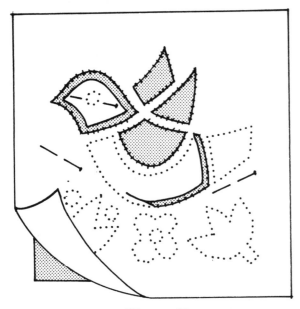

Diagram 36                           Diagram 37

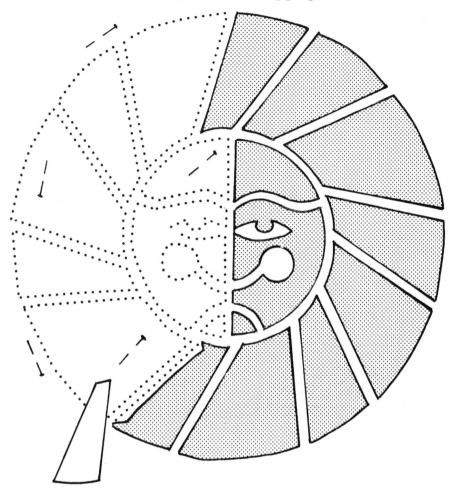

Diagram 38

over it. I added a wide border of navy cotton around the edge and placed quilt batting between the border and the vest for a padded look on the border only. I then drew my designs over the outside and used reverse appliqué, exposing the navy blue, coarse textured lining for contrast. For another bit of interest, I used a turquoise pearl cotton thread for the stitching. This produced larger, more obvious stitches than the usual tiny ones for a little added texture to the motifs (*photo 46*).

This vest features a combination of Seminole Indian patchwork, that was done by Edith Zimmer, and an Indian motif done in reverse appliqué (*photo 47*). The motif came from the book, *American Indian Cut and Use Stencils* by Ed Sibbett, Jr., published by Dover Publications Inc. I traced the motif from the book, transferred it to a dark red fabric and pinned that over a piece of navy blue, matching the colors that Edith used in the patchwork. After

45. Greek style vest

46. Greek style vest (detail)

47. Indian vest combining Seminole patchwork by Edith Zimmer and reverse appliqué motif

56

completing two of these motifs, I made the vest using the appliqué for the two side panels of the vest. If you like Indian designs, that book has many to offer for cut-as-you-go appliqué and reverse appliqué.

This wall hanging, entitled *New Guinea Images* was inspired by another book published by Dover Publications, Inc., entitled *Decorative Art of New Guinea* by Albert Buell Lewis (*photo 48*). Each part was constructed singly in many colors following the spectrum. Each panel is two color reverse appliqué. The panels were not stitched together. They were all stitched to a backing of 1 inch-scale checked gingham. The checks of the gingham served as guideline grids for positioning each panel.

48. *New Guinea Images.* Photo by Sharon Risedorph and Lynn Kellner

Some of the designs vaguely resemble the two color Kuna molas, the ones with narrow channels (*photos 49 and 50*). The others do not, because they contain larger openings that were cut away and they have more unworked space than a mola (*photos 51 and 52*). Whether they are molas or not is immaterial. What matters is that the artist works in the way that feels most comfortable and suitable for the desired effect.

49. *New Guinea Images* detail with similarity to a mola

50. *New Guinea Images* detail with similarity to a mola

51. *New Guinea Images* detail not like a mola

52. *New Guinea Images* detail not like a mola

There are ways of getting more color into a simple reverse appliqué design, if you wish (*photo 53*). Here is the same bird design (*Pattern 5*) done with seven different colors in place of the one color underneath. Instead of pinning one color behind the top layer, try using several by adding each piece one step at a time. It is *not necessary*, as many believe, to use complete layers for each color. It would not only be difficult to cut through so many layers, but it is also too bulky and wasteful of fabric. You need only a small piece for each section of the design. This shows how the back of the design looks (*photo 54*).

This is how it is done: Take a scrap or cut a piece that is large enough to cover the two wings of the bird with ample space around it for pinning (*diagram 39*). Pin it underneath the wings, making sure it is positioned to completely cover the wings underneath. The broken line indicates the edge of the fabric underneath. Cut and stitch the wings. When they are completed, turn the piece over and trim away all the excess fabric about ¼ inch from the stitching (*diagram 40*). Repeat the same process with all the other parts of the design until it is finished. Use as many or as few colors as you wish. You can probably see that this is a good way to use scraps.

53. Pattern 5 with more colors added

54. Back of Pattern 5 with seven colors

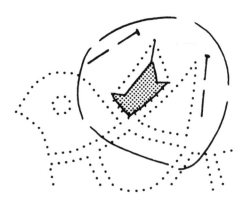

Diagram 39

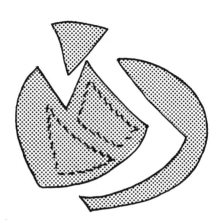

Diagram 40

Another way you might want to try is to make a piece of strip piecing and use it as the underneath fabric (*photo 55*). To create the underneath piece of strip piecing, cut ten strips of different colors to measure 7½ inches by 1¼ inches. Seam them together on the sewing machine with ¼ inch seams. Press the seams in one direction (*photo 56*). Pin this underneath the top layer with the raw edges down and work in the same way, substituting it for the solid underlayer of the two color design. This is the way the back looks with a strip-pieced underlayer (*photo 57*).

55. Pattern 5 with a stripped, pieced under-layer

56. Strips being pieced

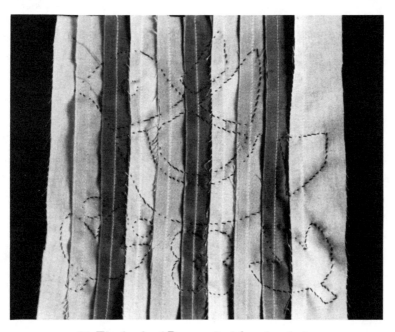

57. The back of Pattern 5 with strip piecing

You may find many interesting ways of using strip piecing with other reverse appliqué designs (*diagram 41*).

This sun design was made entirely of reverse appliqué circles (*photo 58*). The center circle was worked with a solid yellow surrounded by twelve sets of circles in four graduated sizes. Four different prints were used for each of the four sizes of circles. After they were all worked with reverse appliqué, embroidered details were added to complete the design.

Diagram 41

Sometimes it is advantageous to explore different fabrics with textures, prints, stripes or dots for the fabric underneath. You can use almost anything, no matter how coarse (even burlap), for the bottom layer. Since this layer does not have to be cut and folded over for a double thickness, it does not have to be lightweight for manipulating. Just use a fabric that will be functional for the purpose of the project.

For ideas, stencil designs offer a good source of inspiration. Your design must have spaces between the parts at least ¼ inch. Overlapping parts or parts that touch will not work (*diagram 42*). These designs must be adapted to work within the limitations of the technique (*diagram 43*).

I hope I have encouraged you to try a piece of reverse appliqué. I think you will begin to realize why it has become one of my favorite ways of working. In the next chapter we will try a design with a stained glass look, using the same technique.

58. *Sunlight*

Diagram 42

Diagram 43

# 5
# STAINED GLASS
# REVERSE APPLIQUÉ

59. Pattern 6

Achieving a stained glass look in quilts and other kinds of needlework has become a popular trend. Almost everyone responds to the dramatic look of it. It is very easy to create the look of stained glass by using the same reverse appliqué method described in chapter four. The only difference is that only a network of narrow strips of the top layer is left instead of larger solid masses as in *Pattern 5*.

These narrow strips appear as the "leading" of the stained glass. Brilliant colors added underneath the black top layer give the look of bright light shining through colored glass.

This technique is much faster than regular appliqué. After the design is traced on the top layer, there is no need to trace all the parts to the individual colored fabrics and no need to position them. Once the design is traced, all the positioning is complete and there is no further need to trace.

# Pattern 6

Materials: 9 inch square of dark plum cotton broadcloth; small scraps of yellow, orange, burnt orange, red, magenta, fushia and purple; plum thread (For a stronger effect, you may want to substitute black for dark plum.)

1. Trace the pattern to a piece of typing paper. Tape the paper over the page and trace with a pencil.

2. Center the traced pattern over the dark plum square, and pin. Place dressmaker's carbon paper (white or a light color) between the pattern and the fabric, with the carbon side down on the fabric. Trace the design with a wheel or hard pencil. Remove the paper.

3.  Position a small piece of yellow behind the upper portion of the body of the butterfly. Be sure the piece is large enough to pin it outside the body and that it covers the body completely from behind (*diagram 44*). The broken line indicates the edge of the underneath fabric.

4.  Turn it over to the front and pierce the body with the tip of your scissors. Cut the inside of the body with an allowance of ⅛ inch. Clip the corner and curved edges (*diagram 45*).

5.  Fold the edges under and stitch all around.

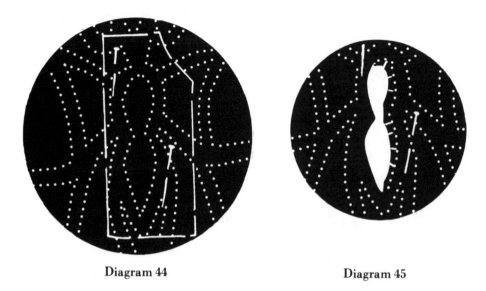

Diagram 44                              Diagram 45

6.  Complete the stitching (*photo 60*). Turn the design over and trim away the excess fabric ¼ inch from the stitching (*photo 61*).

7.  Continue working in the same manner adding yellow to the lower body, burnt orange to the inner portions of the wing next to the body and red to the outer portions of the wing (*photo 62*). This shows the left wing with these colors in place and the right one with the burnt orange partially stitched (*photo 62*). This shows the back (*photo 63*).

8.  Continue, adding purple to the circles in the upper wings, magenta above the butterfly and in the lower corners, and fushia on the sides and below the butterfly. When the design is finished this is how it will look on the back (*photo 64*).

9.  Press as described in chapter one, making sure all the underneath edges are flat. Mark seam lines on the back to form an 8 inch square. Measure ½ inch seam allowance, mark it and trim on the allowance. The design is now ready to piece to the other squares.

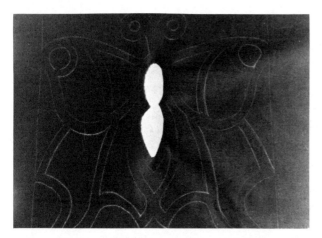

60. Pattern 6, upper body completed

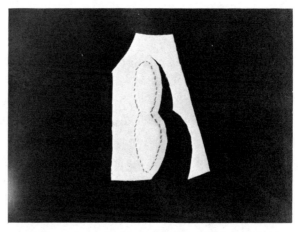

61. Pattern 6, upper body being trimmed on back

62. Pattern 6, left wing with two colors complete, right wing partially worked

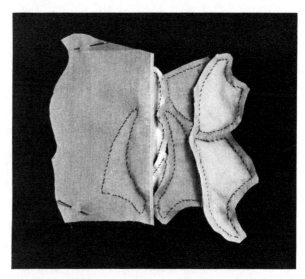

63. Pattern 6, left wing with two colors complete, right wing partially worked on the back

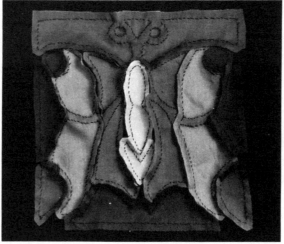

64. Pattern 6, complete back

These four wall hangings were made with this stained glass technique. All have a top layer of black (*photo 65*). This hanging is made of six panels each measuring 8 inches square. The designs are made of all colors of the spectrum. The lattice strips separating them were made of a dull olive green which is a good neutralizing color, meaning that it does not detract from or interfere with the other bright colors.

This hanging was created from four panels measuring 11 inches by 15 inches (*photo 66*). The colors range from gold, yellow, orange, red, magenta to purplish reds and wines with the leaves in shades of green. A purplish red was used for the lattice strips.

65. Wall hanging. Photo by Rick Tang

66. Wall hanging. Collection of Gay Imbach. Photo by Rick Tang

These are two hangings made from two panels each that measure 11 inches by 15 inches (*photo 67*). Each is made up of many shades of greens, golds, oranges, reds, magentas, purples and blues. The borders are magenta.

67. Wall hanging. Photo by Sharon Risedorph and Lynn Kellner

The first time I tried the stained glass look in fabric was on a commission for a church. I was asked to make a funeral pall so I decided to adapt two windows of the church that symbolized the Resurrection and the Ascension. I made the two panels for the center of the pall. I used peau de soie for the colored glass portions to give it a mellow luster.

I liked the idea of creating stained glass with fabric so much that I later made this star design. It was originally created to hang at a window for Christmas (*photo 68*). I wanted the light from outside to shine through it. I stretched it on canvass stretcher bars from an artists' supply store. Next I covered the back with white organdy. This helped to obscure the raw edges on the back so they would not be too prominent from the outside of the window, and yet allow the light through. I used cotton broadcloth for the colors. Light coming through fabric dilutes the color. I learned that vivid colored transparent fabrics such as organdy or voile appear very pale when light comes through them. The cotton broadcloth kept its brilliance with the light coming through

**71**

but still carried a rich glow from the light. If a piece like this remained for a long time at the window, it would fade in time, especially if sunlight hit it. Later I framed this work for the wall.

Before I had experimented very much with the stained glass effect in fabric, I had used the same technique in this design, *German Village* (*photo 69*). Instead of using black to achieve the look of leaded glass, I used it to create the feeling of heavy timbers used on much of the quaint architecture in Germany. I handled the village the same way as the stained glass designs. I used fabrics of greens, blues, turquoises and purples under the top layer to become the buildings. When the building section was completed, I appliquéd it to the ochre sky and added the moon using the reverse appliqué.

There are many possibilities for using this technique for "un-stained glass" ideas. The blocks from a quilt entitled *Natureforms* show how I used white as a substitute for the black to achieve a lighter fresh look (*photo 70*). All of the colored fabrics used beneath the white were in many shades of green, yellow, gold, orange, bright pink and red, all with a small dot pattern. The lattice

68. *Christmas Star*                    69. *German Village*

strips were made from a dark brick red dot. My initial approach was to repeat eight designs, measuring 8 inches square. When those began to get monotonous, I decided to do two things to restore my interest. I designed eight new blocks and I decided to use a solid color of dot fabric instead of separate pieces underneath every alternate block (*photo 71*). The use of the solid color dot gave the quilt more solidity and also speeded up the work. There was less time needed to decide on the placement of colors and less cutting and gathering of fabric scraps.

70. *Natureforms*, two quilt blocks

71. *Natureforms*, more quilt blocks

In spite of this, monotony again set in. I decided I could eliminate nine of the blocks by designing a large "medallion" block for the center of the quilt ( *photo 72*). This helped to recapture my enthusiasm knowing I had a fresh new design replacing the repeating ones. This quilt was laid aside many times during its two year period of completion.

When you find yourself getting bored with a large project or find enthusiasm beginning to build for a new project, lay aside the boring one and start the new one. This little vacation may be all you need to recharge your initial interest in the first one. I usually have several projects going at once and feel uncomfortable if I have only one. That way I never waste time trying to force myself to plug away on a long project. If I would do that, my production would slow down and I would get listless and start longing for a major change in my life. Some people feel compelled to finish one project before allowing themselves the pleasure of starting a new one. I believe in working on the job that beckons most. I find that starting a new project is the biggest part of it and the most exciting part. Once it has begun it usually always gets finished, eventually. There are exceptions when I decide that something is not working as I expected. At some point I make the decision that it is not worth pursuing and I either salvage parts that can be used again or I abandon the entire job. For that reason I do not precut the entire quilt in case I decide to stop work on it or change it.

72. *Natureforms*, quilt with medallion

It also pays to have another project waiting in the wings, in case of a major hold-up on a current one. Sometimes a deadline will determine whether or not I can allow myself the pleasure of switching jobs but I usually find that a deadline will spur me to hurry and finish a job so I can start another, well in advance of the deadline.

This striking quilt, entitled *Summer Morning*, ( *photo 73*), was designed by Fay Goldey and made by herself and eleven friends. Groups that get together

73. *Summer Morning* quilt. Designed by Fay Goldey, made by Fleur Bresler, Barbara Eisman, Alice Geiger, Fay Goldey, Alice Hersom, Nancy Johnson, Mary Krickbaum, Frances Parrack, Yoko Sawanobori, Diane Smith, Jeanne Timken and Sandra Tucker. Photo by Sharon Risedorph and Lynn Kellner.

to share their quiltmaking joys often make quilts for each other as a way of affirming their friendships. Dividing a quilt among friends as a friendship quilt is an excellent way to prevent a large quilt from becoming monotonous to make. This quilt is of such a dynamic design, I'm sure monotony was never a problem. Fay wanted to depart from the traditional block method of quilt-making to create an actual window design in fabric. Her friends agreed to try her stained glass designs with reverse appliqué, even though none had tried it before.

The eight oblong portions in the center were distributed to eight quilters, including Fay. She also created the backgrounds for the side borders, split each of them into two sections and gave them to four other quilters to do the appliqué flowers. She then created the top and bottom borders, set the quilt together and quilted it. Each contributor embroidered her name on her section in matching thread so that the signatures did not interrupt the design.

Fay has really enjoyed working with this method of stained glass and has done many beautiful wall panels.

Another way I have used this technique to depart from the stained glass look has been to use printed fabrics instead of solid colors. For this butterfly design I used a dark mahogany instead of black and I used prints in warm shades of yellows, golds, and oranges for the fabrics beneath the top layer ( *photo* 74).

For this bird, I chose a dark teal blue for the outlines and prints of turquoises, bright pink, and red ( *photo* 75). To enlarge it for framing, I used strips of printed fabrics seamed together "log cabin style," around the central panel. An entire quilt could be made combining designs done in this style with favorite pieced patterns.

I have also found uses for stained glass panels on clothing. To dramatize this long dress of a simple style, I made five 8 inch squares in shades of yellows, golds, greens and turquoise ( *photo* 76). I used black for the leading. I pieced them together with strips of the turquoise dress fabric.

One stained glass panel can add interest to a plain vest if you would prefer to simply embellish a ready-to-wear vest rather than construct one yourself ( *photo* 77). I added some trim to the seams of this vest, matching some of the vivid red and orange of the panel.

You could coordinate the decor of a room by making pillows or a quilt to echo an actual stained glass window or lamp. If you have a friend who does stained glass work, you could work together to design windows and matching fabric accents for a room.

74. Stained glass butterfly with prints

75. Stained glass bird design with prints

76. Stained glass dress

77. Stained glass vest

**77**

# Hints

1. There are many good books on stained glass designs. Dover has published many with good ideas to adapt.
2. To work out a design, use a wide-nib felt pen. One of the dangers in designing is trying to get too much tiny detail. By using a wide pen, this tendency is lessened.
3. I like to use a tracing paper pad, doing several sketches consecutively, slipping each under a new sheet and refining the sketch each time.

Diagram 46, decorative design ideas

# 6
# POSITIVE AND NEGATIVE APPLIQUÉ

78. Pattern 7 (positive)

79. Pattern 7 (negative)

Now that you have learned about cut-as-you-go appliqué with or without cut-outs and reverse appliqué, the next step is combining them. Sometimes I take the same design and do it in both appliqué and reverse appliqué. I call this combination *positive and negative appliqué*. As I mentioned before, I like to get variety in my work, so it never gets dull.

I have used positive and negative appliqué mostly within quilts, because a quilt usually requires repetition of many blocks. I don't like boredom to keep me from finishing a large project—I like to find ways of doing many variations, either by using different colors when I repeat the same design or by this method of combining techniques. I find that while I'm working on one block, I can hardly wait to finish it and try it with another variation so I can see how the two look together. Every block is a new surprise. After I get a few blocks made I am anxious to put them together to see if it is going to live up to my expectations. This goes on until I finally have the quilt top together and get my first look at it. The next step is basting it to the batting and backing, putting it in a frame and watching it come "alive" with quilting. The quilting stitches help to emphasize the positive and negative quality of the appliqué.

Let's take this easy design and do it both ways.

# Pattern 7

Materials: one 9 inch square each of red and orange cotton broadcloth; one 7½ inch square each of plum and hot pink cotton broadcloth; plum and orange thread

*Positive appliqué*
1. Trace the pattern to a piece of typing paper. Tape the paper over the page and trace with a pencil.

2. Pin the traced pattern over the plum square, centering it. Place dressmaker's carbon paper (white or a light color) between the pattern and fabric with the carbon side down on the fabric. Trace the design with a wheel or hard pencil. Remove paper.

3. Center the traced plum square over the red one, pin it with two or three pins.

4. With scissors, start cutting around or between the traced shapes, just a little at a time.

5. Fold the edges under and stitch, using the plum thread with small even stitches.

6. Continue cutting and sewing one piece at a time until all are finished (*diagram 47*).

7. Press the design as described in chapter one. Mark seam lines on the back to form an 8 inch square. Measure a ½ inch seam allowance, mark it and trim on the allowance. The design is now ready to piece to the other squares.


*Negative appliqué*

1. Pin the traced pattern over the orange square, centering it. Place dressmaker's carbon paper (dark enough to show on the orange) between the pattern and fabric as in step two above. Continue with step two.

2. Pin the orange square over the hot pink one, making sure the pink one covers the entire design from behind.

3. With your scissors, pierce one of the parts of the design inside the traced line. Cut inside the line with an allowance of ⅛ inch. Discard the cut scrap.

4. Fold the edge under, clipping as necessary, and stitch it under.

5. Continue with all parts of the design. Remember to cut and sew only one part at a time (*diagram 48*).

6. Follow step seven above.


The first quilt I made using this combination is this one, entitled *Reflections* (*photo 80*). As you can see, I also used one of my favorite techniques, the cut folded-paper designs. I cut these designs from paper to sizes that would fit on two sizes of blocks, 8 inch and 10½ inch squares. I used shades of turquoise, jade, magenta, coral, and burnt orange, combining a warm and a cool color for each block. I then chose a deep mahogany to use as fill-in rectangular blocks, to offset the other colors.

I enjoy doing the blocks with cut-outs in negative because it reverses the design and makes all the negative space become positive. I say "enjoy" because

Diagram 47

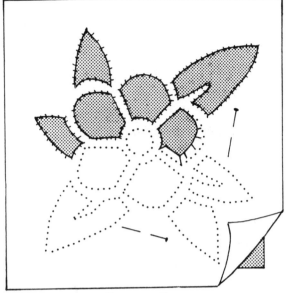

Diagram 48

80. *Reflections* quilt. Photo by Rick Tang

viewers have to stop and figure it out, and I like to play little tricks on people to make them think. We all know that two negatives make a positive. The negative space in a positive design (that is, the space around a figure or shape) becomes positive when the design is reversed to a negative design. In other words, the little heart shaped cut-outs (negative space) in this pattern (*diagram 49*) now become little appliquéd hearts (positive) (*diagram 50*). I call these little bits "islands." Cut-outs of a positive design become "islands" in a negative design.

Just for fun I took the openwork bird pattern, *Pattern 4* and did it as a negative design. All of the little cut-outs now become islands. If you are making all the patterns for the sampler wall hanging you will want to try this too. This time reverse the design to the opposite direction if you are making the wall hanging. Use a 9 inch dark brick red for the top layer to trace the bird on and place a 7½ inch square of orange underneath. Work it as reverse appliqué this time. Use dark brick red thread. The orange bird will be decorated with small flowers of brick red, appliquéd as "islands" over the orange (*diagram 51*).

When quilting positive and negative designs I always put my quilting stitches on the thinner part around the edge of the folded under appliqué. On the positive blocks I stitch around the shape (*photo 81*). On the negative blocks I stitch inside the shape (*photo 82*).

In this quilt, *Twilight*, I took one of my designs for stained glass and

Diagram 49

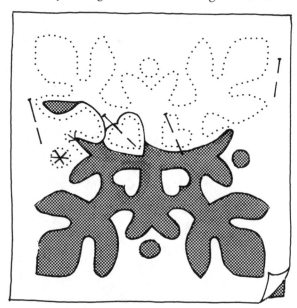

Diagram 50

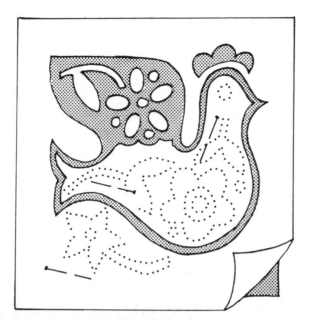

Diagram 51

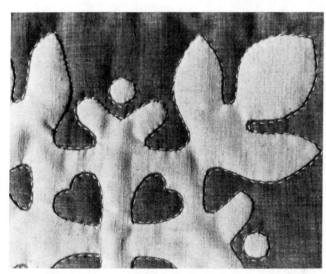

81. *Reflections* quilt (detail positive)

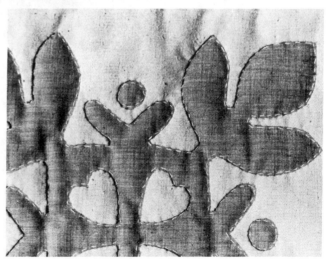

82. *Reflections* quilt (detail negative)

repeated it using dark green with teal and teal with turquoise (*photo 83*). Some of the blocks are positive and some are negative. On four of the blocks I experimented with ways of using three colors together in various forms of negative and positive appliqué. To set the quilt together, I used shades of magenta and orange strips seamed to the two lower edges of each block.

In quilting these blocks, I quilted through the thinner part around the edge of the appliqué. On the blocks with positive appliqué, there is a network of narrow "channels" between the appliquéd parts. In other words, the "leading" of the stained glass now becomes negative space between the solid parts. I quilted within these channels very close to the edge turned under (*photo 84, diagram 52*). In the negative appliqué (reverse appliqué) blocks I quilted within the solid parts (*photo 85, diagram 53*).

83. *Twilight* quilt. Photo by Sharon Risedorph and Lynn Kellner

84. *Twilight* quilt detail (positive)

Diagram 52

85. *Twilight* quilt detail (negative)

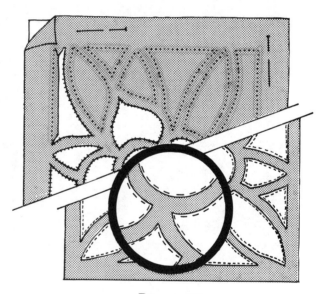

Diagram 53

This quilt, entitled *Dawn*, is made up of eight designs also originally intended for stained glass (*photo 86*). I wanted to use them in a quilt to show how horizontal and vertical rectangular blocks could fit together. I divided the quilt into four major parts. I used very muted shades of green, purple, red, and blue for the four parts. It was a refreshing change to use larger rectangular panels after having used so many squares for quilts before.

To get away from the stained glass look for which they were intended, I chose a lighter color for the narrow outlines and channels and darker colors

86. *Dawn* quilt

for the solid masses. Each of the eight designs appears twice, once in positive and once in negative.

This time I wanted to try another style of quilting. Instead of placing my stitches at the edge as I had in *Twilight*, I placed them ⅛ inch away from the edge. I decided I liked this better. I also found that I could eliminate half of the quilting in the positive blocks by quilting right in the middle of the channels instead of on both sides of them (*photos 87 and 88*). Here is the negative version of both blocks (*photos 89 and 90*). I decided that in the future this is the way I would quilt any similar design.

**88**

87. *Dawn* quilt (detail positive)

88. *Dawn* quilt (detail positive)

89. *Dawn* quilt (detail negative)

90. *Dawn* quilt (detail negative)

This framed design, *Songbirds*, is a mixture of three bird designs done as stained glass, negative, and positive appliqué (*photo 91*). It was done with black and shades of purple, blue, turquoise and green. Patterns for two of these designs are given in this book.

This is a detail of a shirt (*photo 92*). The shirt is a deep wine and the appliqué is blue. The upper man is done as a reverse appliqué on a blue panel at the neckline, allowing the deep wine to show through the blue. The lower one is appliquéd blue on the wine shirt. People often ask if I took the cut away part from the upper figure and stitched it below. That can not be done because there has to be seam allowances. The upper one is slit into narrow channels similar to a mola, so that nothing is really cut and removed. The lower one had to be cut wide enough for allowances.

So far I have shown how to cut and stitch the same design once in positive

91. *Songbirds*

92. Shirt detail (positive and negative)

and once in negative. You can also take one design and do part of it in positive appliqué and part in negative appliqué. Let's take another look at a variation of the sun design from chapter two (*diagram 54*). This time the face of the sun is done in positive (cut-as-you-go) appliqué and the rays are done as negative (reverse) appliqué.

Another possibility for *Pattern* 7 is to do the flower in positive and the leaves in negative (*diagram 55*).

Start looking around for appliqué designs to see how you can vary them with both positive appliqué and negative appliqué.

**90**

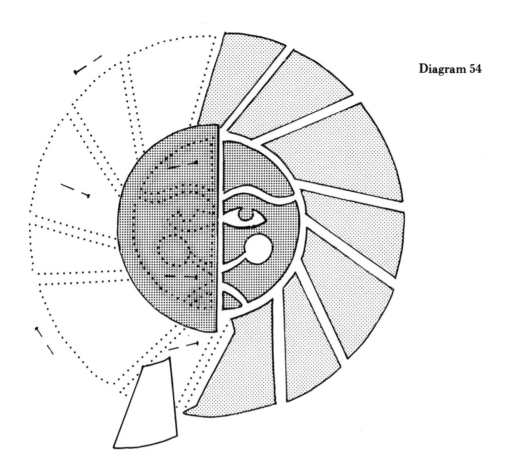

Diagram 54

Diagram 55

91

# MULTI-DEPTH REVERSE APPLIQUÉ

93. Pattern 8

So far in our exploration of reverse appliqué, we have placed the under fabrics beneath the top layer so that only the top layer was cut and stitched. In this chapter, we will add pieces under pieces, to achieve more depth.

It is usually believed and taught that this is accomplished with many complete layers of fabric. When I first started to do reverse appliqué, I followed these directions which stated the necessity of stacking complete layers and cutting through many of them to reach the color you wanted. I tried this on seven or eight projects before I decided that there must be an easier way.

I decided that using multiple layers was wasteful. When I want only one or two small accents of a color, there is no reason to use a complete layer of that color of fabric, most of which served no purpose. I started placing only a small piece where I wanted it to be exposed. When I am working with a favorite color that I can no longer replace, I don't want to waste a scrap of it.

I also found it very frustrating to cut through several layers to reach the color I wanted. It is not a pleasant way to work, either cutting through several layers at once or cutting several layers one at a time. It was very cumbersome and made no sense to me.

I also did not like the result, which was too heavy and bulky. This would never do for a quilt or any other major piece of work of a large size. One of the great advantages of working with fabric is being able to handle, hang, pack, and ship a piece of work easily. I like to keep my work as lightweight as possible, trimming anything away that serves no purpose. I also like to carry the work with me, without needless weight.

Eventually, I decided that most directions written for reverse appliqué had been written by people who had done little or no experimentation but felt the need to repeat what they had read elsewhere. They could not have been written by anyone driven by the joy of doing this wonderful technique!

I began to work with small pieces of fabric only, replacing the solid layers. I like to use as many colors as I want and I don't want to be limited by the number of layers that are practical to baste together. By working with small pieces and scraps I can use as many colors as I want. The end result is much lighter in weight and not bulky. It is more flexible, less wasteful, but best of all it is not aggravating!

Since that departure from the standard directions, I have created hundreds of works with reverse appliqué. There is no end of the exciting effects that can be obtained with many depths of fabrics. This technique is a continuation of what we have already learned about placing a scrap in position, cutting the top, stitching the edge and trimming away all excess fabric.

Let's try this tulip pattern.

# Pattern 8

Materials: 9 inch square of light purple cotton broadcloth; 7½ inch square of orange; 7 inch by 6 inch piece of magenta; small scraps of red, olive and rust; purple, orange, magenta and red thread

1. Trace the pattern on a piece of typing paper. Tape the paper over the page and trace with a pencil.

2. Center the traced pattern over the purple square, and pin. Place dressmaker's carbon paper (white or a light color) between the pattern and fabric with the carbon side down on the fabric. Trace the outer edge of the tulip and the two shapes above it. Do not trace the inner details as this inside of the tulip will be cut away.

3. Pin the square of orange under the purple layer, making sure the entire tulip shape is covered by the orange behind it.

4. With scissors, start cutting inside the traced line with ⅛ inch allowance, folding the edge under and stitching it, cutting as you go.

5. When it is completed, remove the cut away tulip shape and save it for your scrap collection (*photo 94*).

6. Place the pattern over the tulip front and trace the next line inside the tulip (*photo 94*). This will be the next edge to cut and stitch. Sometimes the work shifts position a bit from the original pattern. If this has happened, compensate for it when you trace this line. I find it easier to draw the next part

94. Pattern 8, scrap cut away and next line traced

of the design in freehand when it follows the original line in a similar way. It should be about ½ inch away from the purple edge.

7. Turn the work over and trim away the excess fabric (*photo 95*).

8. Place the magenta piece behind the tulip and pin it in position, making sure all the inner tulip shape is covered from behind (*photo 96*).

9. Cut and stitch inside the traced line on the orange the same as you did before (*photo 97*). Trim the excess fabric from behind.

10. Trace the small details, hearts, flowers, and circles to the front of the magenta piece.

11. Place a red piece of fabric behind the upper middle point of the tulip, beneath the orange piece and work it in the same way, cutting and stitching the orange. Turn it over and trim the excess red.

12. Working only one detail at a time, place small scraps behind, cutting and stitching the magenta for each. The hearts are orange (use part of the cut scrap) the flowers are red, the lower circle and the two circles above the hearts are olive, and the two top circles are rust. Trim each after stitching.

13. The two shapes above the tulip are rust. Place them, cut, stitch, and trim.

14. The circles inside the two flowers are orange. Finish as before. The finished piece will look like this from behind (*photo 98*).

15. Press the design as described in chapter one. Make sure all the under edges are pressed flat. Mark seam lines on the back to form an 8 inch square. Measure a ½ inch seam allowance, mark it and trim on the allowance. The design is now ready to piece to the other squares.

95. Pattern 8, trimming of first fabric back

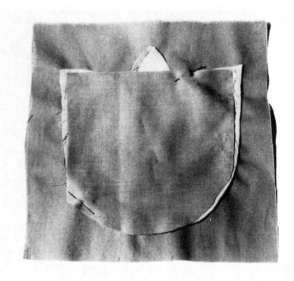

96. Pattern 8, next piece added on back

97. Pattern 8, next fabric being cut and stitched

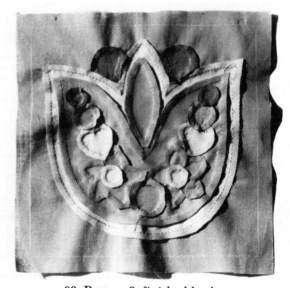

98. Pattern 8, finished back

This is a sign I made to identify my work when it is on display (*photo 99*). It incorporates the logo from my letterhead with many flowers added around it. It has many colors. Most of them were placed directly under the top layer of deep brick red. Some of them have more pieces added, underneath.

This is an example of a design I have used many times as a workshop project

99. Name sign

(*photo 100*). Compare it to the back of the design to understand how it was made (*photo 101*). Later I made this design into a pocket for a tote bag (*photo 102*).

I have used reverse appliqué many times to decorate clothing. The diamond shape on this dress is made of three complete layers (*photo 103*). For a design

100. Reverse appliqué workshop project

101. Reverse appliqué workshop project (back)

102. Tote bag made from workshop pattern.

103. Diamond dress

like this it made sense to use three complete layers instead of small pieces, because the two colors underneath are distributed throughout the design. I traced this design from a bathroom floor tile. While noticing the tile at a friend's house, I realized it was a perfect design for reverse appliqué. I asked my friend for a piece of tracing paper and I traced the design directly from the floor.

The top layer of the diamond is a light steel blue. I traced the design to that around the outer edge only. I placed it over a layer of rust. After the outer edge was completed, I placed a darker steel blue under it and cut and stitched the design again through the rust, revealing the darker blue. I cut the rust ¼ inch from the stitched edge, turned it under ⅛ inch, leaving a ⅛ inch outline between the two blues. This is similar to many mola designs in which the middle layer serves as a narrow outline only.

Much later I designed the dress to accommodate the design. The yoke and sleeves are rust and the main body of the dress is dark steel blue. When I realized the dress needed gussets, I made a pair of mini-diamonds that echoed the large diamond on the front (*photo 104*).

Let's take another look at two of the blocks from the *Sun Friendship Quilt*, shown in chapter two (*photo 105*). This is a block that I made for the quilt to help fill in the gaps needed to complete it. The top layer is yellow. I placed gold under that and worked the edge of the circle. On the gold circle, I traced the points and triangles. Then I used a darker shade of gold under the circle and worked all of those shapes. Under that I added a smaller circle of deep orange for the center of the sun.

One of the most unique blocks of the quilt is this design by Kate Walker (*photo 106*). In this sun block, she began by placing different shades of red and rust squares under the top layer of gold, working one at a time. She cut and stitched each one so that the work resembled a pattern of mosaic tiles. Then she placed a complete layer of bright pink underneath, cut an opening in each square and stitched the edges to reveal the pink within each one. Then she used a narrow bias strip of yellow fabric and stitched it over the mosaic pattern to draw the sun face. This bias strip measured about ⅛ inch when stitched. It was done by cutting a ⅜ inch wide strip on the bias, tucking one edge under ⅛ inch and stitching it, then the other side the same amount (*diagram 56*).

Kate Walker is the only person I know who shares the same love of reverse appliqué that I do. When we met we discovered that we both had preferred

104. Diamond dress (detail)

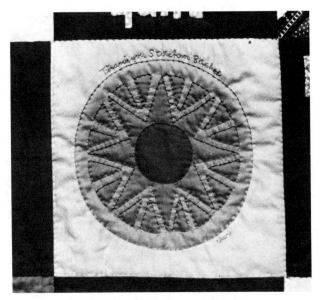

105. *Sun Friendship Quilt* block

106. *Sun Friendship Quilt* block by Kate Walker

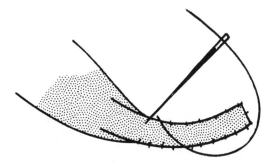

Diagram 56

working with pieces of fabric for the under colors instead of complete layers. She also became very intrigued by the mola techniques and has combined many details from the molas with her own talent and wit to create hundreds of these charming works. She has done some truly remarkable designs in her own inimitable style. I want to introduce other examples of her work.

In this one, entitled *Garden of Eden* (*photo 107*), she traced her design on black cotton, worked all the details with tiny pieces of pink, olive, white, gold, blue, and many other colors. Many of the details have pieces worked under pieces. Then she placed that over black burlap, cut open many spaces to reveal much of the burlap for a contrasting texture (*photo 108*).

This *Unicorn and the Lady* has a top layer of bright pink predominating. It has many small pieces behind it of olive, white, pink, and purple, revealed in

107. *Garden of Eden* by Kate Walker

108. *Garden of Eden* (detail)

all the tiny cut and stitched details (*photos 109 and 110*). This piece reminds me of a Persian garden fantasy.

109. *Unicorn and the Lady* by Kate Walker

110. *Unicorn and the Lady* (detail)

This delightful work, entitled *Everything Under the Sun*, also incorporates the use of black over black burlap. The sun and all the decorative figures are of shades of bright yellows, golds, and oranges, giving it much warmth and cheer (*photo 111*).

*Leo* is one of a series that Kate did on astrological signs (*photo 112*). It is done in gray, black, and magenta. The lion is covered with scattered dots which are tiny openings cut and stitched. This detail is borrowed from the Kuna molas. I admire Kate's perseverance in completing this minute work, which I find very tedious.

I hope you share my enjoyment of Kate's unusual ability to combine a simple, direct, naive approach to her decorative figures with such sophisticated cut and stitch dexterity.

The sun has provided me with an unending source of ideas. This design, entitled *Sun Symbol* was done in two stages (*photo 113*). The first step

111. *Everything Under the Sun* by Kate Walker

112. *Leo* by Kate Walker

113. *Sun Symbol*, collection of Marian Claassen

consisted of forming the underlayer of concentric circles in five graduated shades of gold. I started first with the outer layer, adding a lighter shade under the top layer. I continued the same way with the inner circles ending with the inner circle of pale gold.

I then traced the design for the sun rays to a piece of deep orange cotton. I placed it over the layer of concentric circles and started cutting and stitching, slowly revealing the circles beneath. When that was all completed, I added the facial details with appliqué.

Some designs can become very complex when done in larger sizes. *Mission Church* (*photo 114*), and *Primal Fish* (*photo 115*), may appear that way. Working each detail at a time and adding small pieces behind the openings before adding any complete layers simplifies the procedure. Remember that complete layers serve a purpose when they are seen throughout a design but not when there is only a bit of them exposed.

114. *Mission Church*, collection of Rosalene Bradshaw

115. *Primal Fish*

# Hints

1. Plan your work out on paper first.
2. Do not make the details too tiny or too close together.
3. If your original plan becomes unworkable, make changes as you stitch and adapt to the technique. When a design gets large and complex it is sometimes difficult to think ahead until you actually start working.
4. A larger design is just made up of small designs. Think of only one step at a time.
5. If you should cut a lower piece by mistake, it is easy to replace it with another piece. Sometimes accidents result in good luck and unexpected detail.

# 8
# INLAY APPLIQUÉ

116. Pattern 7

Inlay appliqué is an interesting technique I discovered while exploring some of the molas. There is one mola technique in which one layer of fabric is cut and stitched over another in a series of ½ inch-wide channels. Then another layer is cut to coincide with the channel and appliquéd within it.

I decided that this could also work on larger masses, so I experimented. I chose a traditional tulip quilt pattern and tried it for this pillow (*photo 117*). I traced the design to a black square of fabric and pinned it over a light brown one. I then cut all the shapes out as described in chapter four, and stitched them with simple reverse appliqué.

Using red, orange and green micro-dot fabrics, I pinned these over the parts and traced the shapes to them. I cut them and appliquéd them, within the reverse appliqué shapes, directly to the light brown foundation fabric, allowing the light brown to be revealed in a channel between. I liked the result and it has become one of my favorite ways to create appliqué with another incised look.

Let's try it, using *Pattern 7*

# Pattern 7

Materials: one 9 inch square each of hot pink and burnt orange cotton broadcloth; 7½ inch square of olive green cotton broadcloth; hot pink and olive thread.

1. Trace the pattern to a piece of typing paper. Tape the paper over the page and trace with a pencil.
2. Center the hot pink square over the pattern, pin it, and trace it with a pencil.

117. *Traditional Tulip* pillow with inlay appliqué

3. Center the traced pink square over the burnt orange one and pin. Start cutting and stitching the design as reverse appliqué, just as you did for *Pattern 7*, negative appliqué (*photo 118*).

4. When it is completed, pin the olive square over the flower so all parts of the design are covered (*photo 119*).

5. Now pin a piece of white carbon paper over it with the carbon side against the olive. Flip the whole unit, fabric and carbon paper, over on a table top.

6. Run a tracing wheel inside all the stitched lines (*photo 120*). The image will appear on the olive. When it is traced completely, remove the tracing paper. You now have the image traced on the olive square (*photo 121*).

7. One by one, cut out each shape with a tiny allowance, just a little beyond the traced line. Stitch each shape within the hot pink opening for each, directly to the burnt orange foundation so that about ⅛ inch of the orange shows around each olive piece (*photo 122*).

8. Work all parts until it is finished.

9. Press the design as described in chapter one. Mark seam lines on the back to form an 8 inch square. Measure a ½ inch seam allowance, mark it and trim on the allowance. The design is now ready to piece to the other squares.

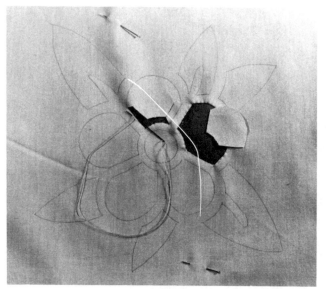

118. Pattern 7, first step reverse appliqué

119. Pattern 7, next layer placed

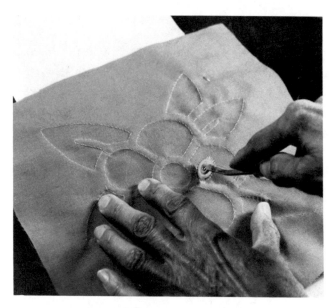

120. Tracing from the back

121. Image traced

While I was making blocks for the quilt, *Twilight*, shown in chapter six, I made one of them with the inlay appliqué technique (*photo 123*). I placed the dark green top layer with the design traced on it over a turquoise square and stitched the design using reverse appliqué. I then placed a teal blue layer over it and inlaid each opening with it. When I quilted it, I placed my stitches within the channel (on the turquoise).

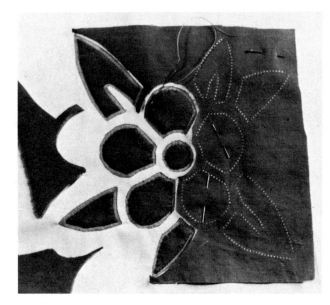

122. Inlaying the third color

123. *Twilight* (detail inlay)

I used a panel of inlay appliqué on the back of this quilted jacket (*photo 124*). The diamond features a layer of rust over a turquoise one, inlaid with purple for the leaves and berries. I added strips of teal, royal blue, purple, magenta, and red around the diamond and finished off the jacket with bright orange and rust in the larger areas. The front pockets echo the diamond design from the back (*photo 125*).

I usually try to keep the channel between the top layer and the appliqué ⅛ inch in width but there is no reason why it can not be as wide as ¼ inch if you prefer (*photos 126 and 127*).

I liked this inlay technique enough to create this dress with a folk art design on the front panel (*photo 128*). I named this dress *Going to the Festival*. The design was inspired by a small terra cotta plaque purchased in Delphi, Greece.

I made the panel of the dress brown over a black foundation. I cut all the shapes from the brown, revealing the black (*photos 129 and 130*). Notice the ten "islands" of the brown background top layer. I used the micro-dot fabric in shades of pink, orange, red, coral, and green to inlay all the detail (*photo 131*). The inlay shapes for a design like this have to be traced partly from the worked parts as described in steps four and five of the directions, and partly from the original pattern where they interlock with each other and don't coincide with the brown edges. A piece of this size usually shifts too much from the original pattern to use it for all the shapes within. Each has to be cut to fit as the work

124. Quilted jacket with inlay appliqué diamond (back)

125. Quilted jacket with inlay appliqué diamond (front)

126. Inlay appliqué diamond

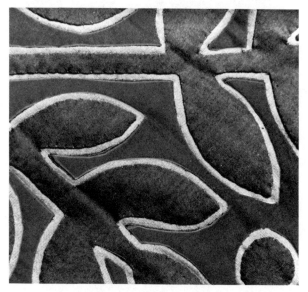

127. Inlay appliqué diamond (close up)

progresses. When the appliqué was complete, I embroidered the small facial details in the two figures with thread. The dress itself is black.

There is another way to do inlay appliqué if two matching designs with the colors transposed are useful (*photo 132*). This is another technique derived

128. "Going to the Festival" dress with inlay appliqué panel

129. First step of reverse appliqué partly worked

130. First step of reverse appliqué, completed

130-A. Second step, adding inlay pieces

131. *Going to the Festival* dress, detail

from the Kuna Indian molas without all the additional filling of space. It is a good way to work if you want to make repetitive patterns for a quilt. The Kunas use it because they use two panels to make their blouses. I call this *Tandem Inlay Appliqué*. It is becoming my newest way to enjoy appliqué. It is the only technique in this book that requires precutting and basting.

# Pattern 9

Materials: one 9 inch square each of purple and turquoise cotton broad-cloth; two 9 inch squares of orange cotton broadcloth; purple and turquoise thread

1. Trace the pattern on a piece of typing paper. Tape the pattern over the page and trace with a pencil.

132. Pattern 9, tandem inlay appliqué

2. Center the traced pattern over the purple square and pin. Place dress-maker's carbon (white or a light color) between the pattern and fabric with the carbon side down on the fabric. Trace the pattern. Remove the paper (*photo 133*). On the left is my original felt pen pattern.

3. Pin the traced purple square over the turquoise square.

4. Cut on the lines (*photo 134*). This is the only time that I do not tell you to

133. The pattern traced on the top piece

add an extra allowance. Cut through both of the layers of fabric. Cut around the butterfly only. Do not cut around the body or the antennae yet.

5. Separate the four pieces (*photo 135*). Place them on top of the orange squares, transposing the colors so that the purple butterfly is surrounded by turquoise and the turquoise butterfly is surrounded by purple.

6. Baste all pieces.

134. Two layers cut simultaneously

135. Four pieces separated

7. Start with the background at the top of the butterfly, turning the edge under ⅛ inch and stitching it down (*photo 136*).

8. Cut the two slits for the antennae and stitch under each edge.

9. When the background with the antennae is completed, cut and stitch the body of the butterfly in place.

10. Stitch around the body and wings. Remove basting. You should now have a butterfly defined by a channel of orange.

11. Repeat with the other piece.

12. Press the designs as described in chapter one, page 15. Mark seam lines on the back to form an 8 inch square. Measure ½ inch seam allowance, mark it and trim on the allowance. The design is now ready to piece to other squares or whatever you want to make.

Two designs like this can be used, one above the other, for a dress or shirt. They could also be used on each side of a tote bag or for a pair of matching pillows. Or you may want to begin a quilt with them, adding other simple designs and the same technique for the other blocks.

I have begun a series of tandem inlay appliqué blocks which I am using for my next quilt, which I will name *Skylark* (*photo 137*).

136. Four pieces basted and outer edge being stitched

137. Two tandem inlay appliqué blocks

# 9

# FINISHING

138. *Cutwork Appliqué* wall hanging. Photo by Sharon
Risedorph and Lynn Kellner

If you have completed all the exercises in this book and want to make the wall hanging, it needs to be finished off. The finished size is 30 inches by 38 inches.

Materials: 12 squares of appliqué; border strips of deep magenta of any preferred fabric, two 3½ inches by 33 inches and two 3½ inches by 30 inches; binding strips of gold cotton broadcloth, two 2¼ inches by 38 inches and two 2¼ inches by 31 inches; a backing of any desired fabric 30 inches by 38 inches; one sleeve strip of any of the above fabrics 4 inches by 29 inches; magenta thread; a rod. (If you prefer to quilt your wall hanging, you'll need a piece of quilt batting the same size of the backing).

1. Seam the squares together as shown in the photograph. Seam three together for each row and press the seams in the same direction. Seam the four rows together and press the seams flat.

2. Seam the longer magenta strips to the sides of the hanging and press the seams outward. Seam the remaining two strips to the top and bottom and press the seams outward.

3. Baste the whole piece to the backing. If you are using quilt batting, insert it between the layers before basting.

4. Quilt around the edge of each square. If you are using batting, you may also want to quilt around each appliqué edge.

5. Seam the longer gold strips to the front sides of the hanging and press the seams outward. Fold ½ inch from the seam and press to the back of the hanging. Stitch the back of the binding to the back of the hanging by hand, turning the edges under. Press.

6. Seam the remaining gold strips to the front top and bottom. Press and stitch the same way. Finish off the ends by hand turning them to the inside. Press.

7. Attach the sleeve across the top back by hand, turning the edges under.

8. Insert rod.

There are certain questions that I am frequently asked. I will try to answer them:

Q. How do you get so much done?

A. I never seem to get enough done, but I use the shortcuts in this book. I try to work the simplest way I can, eliminating anything that seems unnecessary to me. I take work with me wherever I go and try to use all of my time.

Q. Where do you get your fabrics?

A. When I hear that question I think the person who asks hopes I will name one magic source that has it all, in order to avoid frustrating shopping trips. Although there are excellent shops, many favorites, no one shop has everything at one time. I usually never go out shopping for anything special. I drop in on shops when I am nearby and wherever I travel. The fabrics just beckon me. It takes years of collecting. Colors come and go, in and out of fashion, and the selection never stays the same. Fabric shop owners really try to provide everything possible for their customers but they are limited by what is manufactured. It would be wonderful to find a shop that stocked every color of the spectrum in every shade in the weight that I like to use, but that is a dream.

Q. How did you learn to use color? Is it a natural ability one is born with or can anyone learn?

A. I took color classes in school but all I can remember is learning words like primary, secondary, tertiary, etc.

I remember in the late 50s my awareness of color suddenly changed. I think the whole world of design had new attitudes about color. Suddenly colors we had learned never should go together started going together—purple, red, orange. Purple and orange had barely existed before. I worked in Chicago then and my apartment was decorated in earth colors—safe and subtle—gold, russet, green, brown. I then moved to San Francisco and started over. This time I used green, turquoise and blue with a bath of pink and orange. Colors I had never thought about before.

Q. Can a color sense be developed or is it just natural for some that are born with it?

A. I don't know if it can be learned. I know my attitude about color changed and I think others can change theirs too. I think it is a matter of awareness. When you see a color scheme that excites you, copy it, make a note of it, pay attention to your own feelings about it.

I have strong feelings about color. I prefer clear bright colors, but they can be very gaudy and out of control when used improperly. They need to be neutralized by muted colors or dark colors. Amish quilts do this. How did the Amish have such a sophisticated feeling for color?

I like muted "dirty" colors also. My favorites for neutralizing bright colors are olive, bronze, brick red and plum. By "neutralizing" I mean colors that give my favorite bright colors a "fair shake." They don't intrude but they give the bright colors equal opportunity. I always like backgrounds to be dark or muted.

I am not comfortable with pastel colors. I find them difficult to work with, yet when I see contemporary quilters like Michael James using graduated color schemes—light through dark—I am fascinated! I feel like going out to look for pastels. They look best blended with darker shades of their hues in a color mix. When I designed embroidery for kit production I was always frustrated when told to use the colors that "sell." These were usually pastels. I could not work with them.

There are certain colors I must have on my fabric shelf. These are shades of magenta and turquoise. Sometimes people do a lot of designs with rainbows. They usually use yellow, orange, red, purple, blue, and green. I think this needs magenta between red and purple, and turquoise between blue and green. It ties the spectrum together better—otherwise it looks "raw." If you buy a box of 10 felt pens, they always include a magenta or hot pink and a turquoise. This feels good to me.

I like to use many closely-related shades of a color such as a magenta, red, and vermillion. When I worked as a graphic artist, there was always a limit on the number of colors that could be used. Each color printed adds to the cost of the job, so I was usually limited to two or three colors. One problem that occurs when your project is to be photographed and printed is choosing colors that separate from each other. Printing of a photograph often makes subtle color variations invisible and they come out looking like one solid color. You must think about this when your work is for publication.

Colors feel discordent if they don't relate well. There must be a relationship that brings them together. For example, a yellow with a lemon cast will clash with a purple with a bluish cast. To unite them, choose a yellow with a bit of orange in it and a purple with a bit of red. Yellow and purple are hard to use together because yellow is the lightest color in the spectrum and purple is the darkest. This places them too far apart. For that reason I use gold more than I use yellow in my designs. Gold is not as difficult to place with other colors. Yellow looks good with its own family of gold, orange, and yellow-green but it looks out of place with colors that are darker in their pure state.

I always like to arrange my colors following the spectrum, whether they are fabrics, yarns, paints, pencils, or felt pens. Then I know exactly what I have to work with.

Q. Do you ever agonize over choosing a color?

A. Only when a certain color I need is missing from my shelf. That's why I like to buy fabric when I see it so I have it handy when the creative urge strikes. One thing that is agonizing at times is selecting a color for a border for a quilt or hanging made up of many colors and values of blocks. Trying to find the right color that gives all the other colors equal contrast is not easy.

Q. How do you know how much fabric to buy if you don't have a definite use in mind?

A. That is difficult to answer. It depends on many things: what I think I might do with it, how I feel about it, how far from home the shop is (if I will not pass that way again and it is a hard-to-find favorite, I might buy 5 yards, if the shop is in my town I might buy ½ yard), whether or not it is a current fashion color (will it sell out next week or will it be around for several seasons?). If I don't guess right and run out of a color when I need it, I have the interesting challenge of figuring out another alternative.

Q. What is your favorite color and what color do you hate?

A. I like so many colors I don't really have a favorite. Certain ones become favorites, then they fade away and others take their place. This usually happens with colors I wear. Chartreuse is probably the color I use least, but sometimes it makes a good accent.

Q. Where do you get your ideas?

A. I think they come from an awareness—paying attention to something that catches my eye and causes a feeling of excitement. I save things—greeting cards, magazine clips, gift wrap paper, travel folders. I find the act of cutting them out and filing them in my cabinet keeps it somewhere in my unconscious. When I need it, it surfaces and I pull it out of the file. I also take a lot of pictures. I can pull out slides of Swiss posters, a Canadian milk carton, or a piece of Greek embroidery. I also have shelves of books. The idea is not to copy these things but to look at them and let them trigger new ideas.

I think most people get feelings of excitement when they look at certain things but they don't make an effort to remember it: *pay attention to those little exciting feelings!*

# I USED TO BE AN OUTDOOR GIRL

I used to be an outdoor girl . . . .
Pine needles in my tent
But now I cut and then I sew
Until my needle's bent

The alpine flowers miss my step,
The chipmunks now don't know me.
The redwoods tall, the mountain peaks
Their splendors seldom show me.

I used to be an outdoor girl.
New interests now conflict.
The old ones beckon all the while
Force new ones to constrict.

I choose to stay with appliqué
Discovering new delight!
With pattern, color I design
A new way to excite.

I used to be an outdoor girl
I skied and hiked the meadow
But now I trace and cut and sew
Here in my fabric ghetto.

# INDEX

Pattern 1

Pattern 2

Pattern 3

134  Pattern 4

Pattern 5

136                          Pattern 6

Pattern 7

Pattern 8

Pattern 9

Additional Stained Glass Appliqué Pattern

Additional Stained Glass Appliqué Pattern

Additional Reverse Appliqué Pattern

Additional Reverse Appliqué Pattern

144              Additional Reverse Appliqué Pattern

Ideas for uses

Ideas for uses

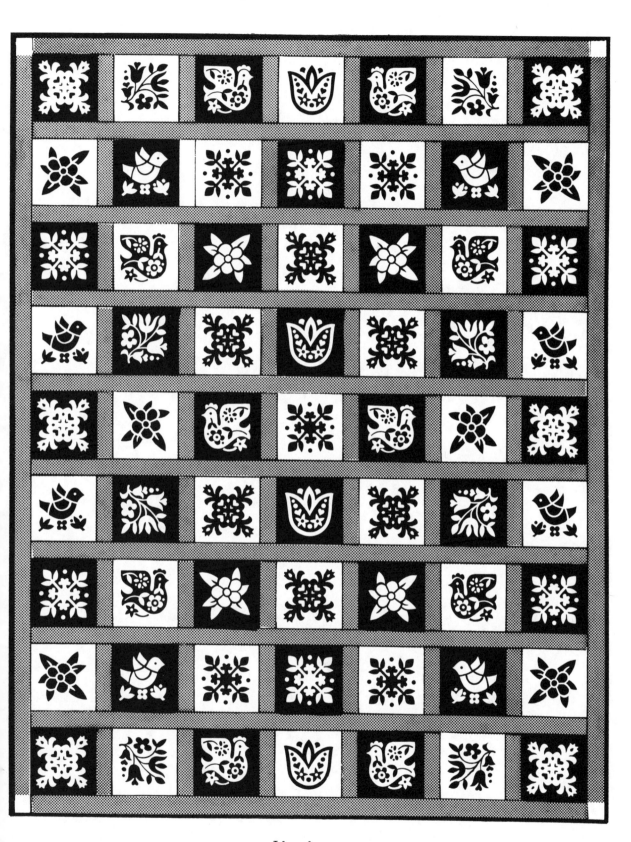

Ideas for uses